The Evidence
for
PHANTOM HITCH-HIKERS

An objective survey of the Phantom Hitch-Hiker phenomenon
in all its manifestations.

The Evidence for PHANTOM HITCH-HIKERS

MICHAEL GOSS

Series Editor: Hilary Evans

THE AQUARIAN PRESS
Wellingborough, Northamptonshire

First published 1984

398.21
G

© MICHAEL GOSS 1984

British Library Cataloguing in Publication Data

Goss, Michael
    The evidence for phantom hitch-hikers.
    1. Hitchhiking—Folklore   2. Ghosts—Folklore
    I. Title
    398.2'1   GR75.H5

    ISBN 0-85030-376-1

*The Aquarian Press is part of the
Thorsons Publishing Group*

Printed and Bound in Great Britain by
Whitstable Litho Ltd, Whitstable, Kent

CONTENTS

'THE EVIDENCE' Series is prepared by the Aquarian Press in collaboration with ASSAP (Association for the Scientific Study of Anomalous Phenomena) under the editorship of Hilary Evans. Each book is written by a recognized authority on the subject who is in a position both to give a comprehensive presentation of the facts and to analyze them in the light of his own experience and first-hand research.

———————————————— ● ————————————————

ASSAP (Association for the Scientific Study of Anomalous Phenomena) was founded in 1981 to bring together people working in different fields of anomaly research. It does not compete with other societies or organizations, but serves as a link organization enabling members of existing groups to share views and information and benefit from pooled resources. ASSAP issues its own publications, has its own research archives, library and other facilities, and holds periodic public conferences and training events in various parts of the country: ASSAP co-operates with local groups or, where none exists, may form one of its own.

ASSAP members include people from all walks of life who share a belief that it is the scientific approach which is most likely to solve these enigmas: they are neither uncritical 'believers' on the one hand, nor blinkered sceptics on the other, but are ready to go where the evidence leads them. If you sympathize with this attitude and would like to participate actively in our exciting pursuit of the truth, you may consider joining us. Write for fuller details to the Editor, Evidence Series, Aquarian Press, Denington Estate, Wellingborough NN8 2RQ.

ILLUSTRATIONS

Cover: Illustration of typical Phanton Hitch-Hiker by Belinda Evans.

ACKNOWLEDGEMENTS

The author would like to thank the following people and organizations for their assistance:

For background on the Nunney case: Mrs Bane (Frome Public Library), local historian Mr Michael McGarvie, Frome Police, Mr Owen Hillier, Mr Fred L'Estrange, Mr John Bowman and Wessex Newspapers.

For background on the Stanbridge case: Mr Roy Fulton, Dunstable Police, Mrs Anne Cox (*née* Court) and Mr Bill Stone.

For background on the Blue Bell Hill saga: Mr Tom Harber, Mr Dennis Chambers, Rochester and Maidstone Divisions of the Kent Constabulary, Chief Inspector Clark (Police Dog School, Essex), Inspector Alan Clarke and his son Andrew, Joan Forman, Mr Dick Allen, *Kent Messenger* Information Unit, Chatham Public Library staff.

For general material and advice: Ms Theo Brown, Mr Sam Richards, Watson Library of the Folklore Society (University of London), British Library Newspaper Division (Colindale), Steve Moore and Bob Rickard (*Fortean Times*), Mr Alan Gardiner, Mr Paul Screeton, Mr Melvin Harris, Professor Alvin H. Lawson, Brian and Maggie Duffield and (of course) Mrs Sheila Goss.

For material from non-British publications: Hilary Evans, Bill Zeiser (Indianapolis), Donald K. Johnston (Downey, Cal.), Ms G. M. Gardner (Everett, Washington), Martin S. Kottmeyer (Carlyle, Ill.), Chris Holtzhausen (Pretoria, SA), Jacob Davidson (editor of *Full Moon*, Hawaii), the editors of *Fate Magazine*, D. Scott Rogo, Mr and Mrs Clay Hall and Mr Chaw Mank, Sven Rosen for the Swedish (J. P. Klint) account of c.1602-08, A. Arnold (Swiss material).

For translations from French: Mrs Margaret Duffield (*merci*!).

In memoriam: a belated expression of thanks to Mr Brian C. Nisbet (d.1981) for several years' sound advice, encouragement and scrutiny of an early draft of this book.

For permissiom to quote from copyright material the author is grateful to:

Gerald Duckworth and Co. Ltd. for permission to quote passages from

Alfred Sutro's *Celebrities and Simple Souls* (1933), pp.227-229. The Folklore Society for permission to quote from Andrew Lang's '"Death's Deeds": A Bilocated Story', in *Folklore* XVIII No. 4 (31 December 1907), pp.376-390; B. T. Batsford Limited for permission to quote from Kingsley Palmer's *The Folklore of Somerset* (1976), p.136; Victor Gollancz Ltd. for permission to quote from Charles Fort's *Lo!* (1931), p.90; Hulton Educational Publications Ltd for permission to quote from 'The Devil and the Coachman', in S. H. Atkins' *Ballads Old and New* (1968), pp.21-23; The Editors of *Fate Magazine* for permission to quote from Cecil de Vada's 'The Phantom Hitchhiker', in the issue for August 1968, pp.86-90; Ms Joan Forman for permission to quote from her *The Haunted South* (Robert Hale and Co., 1968). Material from Aniela Jaffé's *Apparitions and Precognition* (New York: University Books, 1963) appears by arrangement with Lyle Stuart, Inc. of Secaucas, New Jersey; the extract from Ernest Baughman's *The Type and Motif-Index of the Folk-Tales of England and North America* (Indiana Folklore Series No.20, 1966), pp.147-149, appears by permission of Mouton Publishers (Division of Walter de Gruyter and Co.); the Editors of *Western Folklore* for permission to quote from the *California Folklore Quarterly* papers of Richard K. Beardsley and Rosalie Hankey (October 1942, January 1943) and Louis C. Jones (October 1944); W. W. Norton and Co. Inc. for permission to quote from Jan Harold Brunvand's *The Vanishing Hitchhiker. Urban Legends and Their Meaning* (1983).

ONE: THE PHANTOM HITCH-HIKER
a much-travelled ghost

One Friday night in October 1979 duty officers at Dunstable Police Station heard a highly unusual – some would say sheerly incredible – story from a 26-year-old carpet fitter named Roy Fulton.

A subsequent chapter will describe how Mr Fulton broke his journey homeward from a darts match to offer a lift to a pale-faced young man whom the car headlamps revealed at the roadside, thumb upraised in the customary hitch-hiker's gesture, near the village of Stanbridge. The ride ended minutes later when he discovered that the strangely silent passenger had vanished, imperceptibly and illogically, from the seat beside him as the Mini van cruised at a steady 45 m.p.h.

This was the germ of the story told by Mr Fulton almost immediately afterwards over a much-needed large Scotch in his local pub, whose landlord Bill Stone was quoted by the *Sunday Express* of the 21 October 1979 as deeming the witness to be '"a rough and ready, happy-go-lucky sort of lad"', who '"wouldn't make up stories like that"'. Highly unusual, sheerly incredible as it may have seemed, the same story and the evident sobriety of the person telling it persuaded the police to initiate a futile check-cum-search of the area where the incident was alleged to have taken place. Inspector Rowland's published response provided the *Express* journalist with a natural and perfect conclusion for what was a first-class 'spooky' tale. '"We hear strange things from people,"' he affirmed, '"but there aren't too many ghost stories like this one."'[1]

Accurate as the Inspector's assessment of the story's rarity value may be in connection with Dunstable, it scarcely applies to the rest of the country, and far less to the whole world. Indeed, bar the important omission of a satisfactory conclusion – one that explains for us the assumed-ghost's identity – Roy Fulton's account is typical of a perennially-repeated narrative, one told and retold all over the globe: the Phantom Hitch-Hiker.

The Phenomenon

The Phantom Hitch-Hiker (better known in the USA as the Vanishing Hitchhiker) is nothing short of being a classic ghost story. In advance of the interrelated themes pursued throughout this study a few definitive statements can be set down serving to justify its claim to that status. As a matter of priority, however, let the following outlines serve as an introduction to the much-travelled ghost. They are based upon stories published by national newspapers in the decade to which the Fulton account belongs and all will be summarized more adequately at later points in the text.

Sassari, Sicily (1973): Noticing the strange coldness of a girl who hitched a ride on his motorcycle, factory worker Luigi Torres lent her his overcoat. On reaching her house he told her he would collect it next day. When he called to do so he was shocked to learn his passenger had been dead for three years. On the girl's grave Luigi found both a photo of the Hitch-Hiker he had encountered the night before *and* his overcoat.

Greifnau, Germany (1975): A 43-year-old businessman picked up 'a weird looking woman dressed in black' who 'murmured that something evil would happen. When I looked next she had vanished.'

Peshawar, Pakistan (1979): Police motorcyclist Mahmood Ali gave a lift to a pretty girl in white who vanished before reaching the destination to which she had asked to be taken. A photograph of a 20-year-old victim of a fatal road accident was found to match the Hitch-Hiker 'eyelash by eyelash'.[2]

Here is a highly typical Hitch-Hiker tale condensed from an undated (1968?) account produced by an oral informant:

Motoring on the road between Chatham and Maidstone one night at around 11 p.m., a man saw a girl in her early teens thumbing a lift at the crest of Blue Bell Hill. She asked to be taken to Maidstone and during the ride mentioned her address in that town; speaking almost continuously in what the motorist felt was a state of high excitement, she also announced that she was to be married the next day. On reaching the outskirts of Maidstone her conversation lapsed and the driver was startled to discover she had unaccountably vanished from the car; he had not noticed the passenger door opening and had been keeping to a moderately high speed as they travelled. Although he gradually rationalized that the girl must have slipped out unseen when the car slowed down in heavy traffic, he was concerned about her safety and proceeded to the address which the girl had let slip during the conversation. Here he was told by the girl's mother that (X) –

obviously identical with his talkative passenger – had been killed in a car crash on Blue Bell Hill. This tragic event had taken place on the eve of her wedding three years ago to the very day and hour he had met the Hitch-Hiker.

We can now move to an analytical consideration of what Inspector Rowland was quoted as regarding as a story unique to Dunstable. First we may assert that:

– Viewed purely in terms of construction, the basic narrative line or plot is strikingly simple. As in the Fulton account, an unaccompanied driver picks up a hitch-hiker who in due course vanishes from the speeding vehicle. Unlike the Dunstable episode, however, the more polished versions include a sequel: the Hitch-Hiker prefaces the act of disappearance by providing (in an oblique way) evidence through which the witness can confirm that he was in contact with an authentically supernatural being. Usually this takes the form of the Hitch-Hiker mentioning an address to which the witness proceeds, only to learn that the vanishing passenger can be clearly identified as a person deceased for some period of time. Other forms of corroboration might derive from the Hitch-Hiker borrowing an overcoat or comparable garment which the witness later reclaims. The encounter may well take place on the aniversary of the Hitch-Hiker's demise.

– As sketched above (though with a variety of localized or individual minor departures) this story occurs in practically every country in the world. It is not too much to say that wherever there are roads there are likely to be variants of the Hitch-Hiker narrative. Although some major populated countries may seem exceptions to this generalization – the USSR, parts of South America, New Zealand – it is quite likely that relevant material has simply escaped the attention of the (mainly) English-speaking researchers who collect and classify Hitch-Hiker accounts, perhaps through unfamiliarity with the language and publications of the countries concerned.

– More surprising than the Phantom Hitch-Hiker's ubiquity is its *antiquity*. Contrasting sharply with the apparent modernity of the tale as it is usually told today (for example, the strong focus on the motor car as the medium that makes the encounter possible) is a mass of evidence proving that our current versions are updated treatments of a far older motif. These observe the rule by which the supernatural travelling companion always uses the customary transportational mode contemporary with the date of the story, be it horse, wagon or (in Roy Fulton's case) Mini van. Conceivably, the Hitch-Hiker will continue to do so if and when the automobile is superseded by something else.

Constant repetitions of what is essentially the same story ought to lead to rapid decline in the Hitch-Hiker's popularity, yet there is nothing to suggest that it is in danger of losing its audience appeal. Evidently it possesses peculiar attractions which enable it to pose as fresh, unique and amazingly 'different' with each telling. In part, this could be due to the fact that:

– despite its stereotyped core or motif the Phantom Hitch-Hiker is a curiously flexible ghost story; one permitting incorporation of individual details that allow the kind of updating just remarked upon *or* those adapting it to the needs of the storyteller, the expectations of the audience, the socio-cultural heritage of both. Minor changes include deliberate relocation of the tale in a setting known to the circle of listeners/readers and descriptive changes (age, sex, appearance of the Hitch-Hiker, type of conveyance, and so on), but there may also be more dramatic though circumscribed thematic alterations.

– folklorists recognize at least four significant variants of the basic motif. The preceding summaries encapsulate three of these: the conventional address-giving ghost (e.g. Blue Bell Hill), a spirit (?) that utters some sort of prophecy (Greifnau), and another standard deceased spirit that borrows an article of clothing to manipulate as proof (Sassari). We only lack the fourth possibility, where the Hitch-Hiker is a goddess or tutelary being. This leads to the suggestion that:

– the identity of the Hitch-Hiker can be transmogrified according to the prevailing beliefs and dogmas of the particular culture, or a defined sector within a culture against which the story is set.

The Hitch-Hiker is most commonly interpreted as a pitiable yet benign ghost (as predicated by the generic name, '*Phantom* Hitch-Hiker'): the spirit of a deceased human being, frequently a victim of a tragic road accident. This hardly does justice to its versatility. Cultural contouring – the process by which a phenomenon is interpreted in the light of a specific concensus pattern – allows the Hitch-Hiker to support whatever message of enlightenment or doom fits group circumstance. Thus, without contradiction, it is an angelic prophet for Mormons and Catholics in the USA, a vampire in Malaysia, a native deity on Hawaii and a vaguely-Christianized agent of apocalypse in countries as far apart as southern Sweden and northern Italy.

So far we have surveyed the Phantom Hitch-Hiker as a wholly fictive ghost: one which only simulates a genuine, real-life event. As such it conforms to the established literary convention of the 'true' supernatural tale where the narrator attempts to *temporarily* create a suspension of disbelief by recounting something beyond the normal bounds of possibility under the guise of an authentic *personal* experience – *or* as that of an absent person for whose unimpeachable veracity he will swear. This corroboration is meant to be accepted uncritically. Convention demands that we do not challenge the speaker when he insists that the impossible happened to him, or disallow the story simply because the speaker cannot produce the friend of a friend to whom it purportedly happened. In a word, the story is anecdotal and the 'evidence' (the good faith of the narrator) is not to be questioned scientifically.

Acknowledging the sheer volume of Phantom Hitch-Hiker stories – the 100-plus upon which this present book draws is far from an exhaustive sample – and the formidable geographical distribution of the motif, a detailed review of the material in terms of folklore or popular fiction is justifiable. But there is more to the matter than this, since the factual basis of the story does not entirely rest upon the lightly-rendered, easily-digested kind of corroboration just discussed. When we come upon the 'personal experience' technique in a book of transparently fictional ghost stories we seldom have difficulty in recognizing it at once for the narrative device it is. Problems arise when something closely comparable appears in a source we are prone to think is *not* devoted to fiction, but to the literal truth: the newspapers.

As stipulated earlier, the Hitch-Hiker received special attention from the world's press during the 1970s, culminating in the *Sunday Express* reports of the Fulton episode and (just a few weeks later) the pretty girl in white who bemused a novice policeman outside Peshawar, Pakistan. These articles were submitted for the public's attention in the shape of hard news items befitting the contents of national newspapers. In precisely the same fashion the popular magazine *Weekend* published as a reader's true-life adventure Mr Cedric Davidson-Acres' tale of an attractive Malaysian Hitch-Hiker encountered by him on a road through lush forests leading to the Jambataan Merdeka bridge over the Kedah River.[3] Accepting the offered lift with a smile (the narrator did not find her silence odd, as Malay women are traditionally bashful), she took a seat in the back of the car and subsequently vanished amid a strong fragrance of frangipani flowers. Mr Davidson-Acres later heard he was not the first to give a ride to this mystery woman of 'Freedom Bridge'.

Finding these accounts wedged beside other components of news – wars, strikes, trade statistics and other eminently credible items – may encourage readers to see them as reports of strange but true occurrences. If we regard them as over-sophisticated hoaxes or else as flippantly-rendered pieces inserted by way of contrast or light relief, we can only conclude that our newspapers sometimes abandon their much-vaunted regard for 'the facts' and publish material they either suspect or know to be fantasy. This is a serious allegation to which we must return. For the moment we can agree that *at face value*, these media reports appear to be assuring us that the Phantom Hitch-Hiker is a phenomenon that repeatedly manifests itself across the world. Against this stands the coequal fact that the most reliable-sounding testimonies to the truth from narrators whose word would carry utmost conviction were they testifying on matters remote from the paranormal need to be treated with considerable circumspection.

Playwright Alfred Sutro, the man whose translations introduced the work of Maeterlinck to English audiences, would have enjoyed comparing notes with Messrs Fulton and Davidson-Acres. In his reminiscences, which appeared under the title of *Celebrities and Simple Souls* a few days after his death on 11 September 1933, he related his single 'psychic experience; rather mysterious, and bewildering; and a creepy feeling comes over me as I tell of it'.[4] Motoring on a lonely country road a little above a stream half-hidden by trees, he heard the wail of a child. Despite his chauffeur's inability to share that impression (the man was 'inclined to be deaf, besides being rather a surly and ill-conditioned fellow'), Sutro clambered down to the river bank, where he discovered 'a pretty little girl, of three or four, crying and sobbing'. The child would not be comforted, but allowed herself to be carried back to the car. She was wringing wet, having 'evidently fallen into the water', and Sutro could not imagine what she was doing in so desolate a place; nor would she interrupt her weeping to talk about it. When the concerned man pointed straight on in the hope of eliciting where she lived, the girl acquiesced with a nod.

A short distance away the girl signalled towards the gate and drive of a 'largish house'. Sutro continues:

I got out, went up some steps, the door was flung open, a man and woman rushed to me. 'Have you any news of the child?'. 'She's in the car,' I said, and they flew past me; I followed; there they were, standing by the car – but it was empty; the child was gone. 'Where's the little girl?' I shouted to the chauffeur. 'Little girl,' he said, staring at me. I cursed the fool. 'The child, the child I brought into the car!'. 'You didn't bring any child into the car,' he said, looking at me as though he thought I was mad.

Driving back to the place on the river-bank where he had discovered the unhappy girl, the author found her dead body lying in four feet of water. He had not carried a human being back to his car, but a ghost. And though she ignored the formality of thumbing for a lift, the Sutro girl nonetheless falls into the behavioural category known to researchers as the Phantom Hitch-Hiker.[5]

Alfred Sutro (1863-1933). This cartoon by Harry Furniss brings out the impish humour that led the playwright to invent a 'true' ghost story, which – he claimed – deceived numerous listeners. (*National Portrait Gallery, London*)

As a story, Sutro's psychic adventure is superior to those of Roy Fulton and Cedric Davidson-Acres. Theirs emerge as baffling, unexplained fragments featuring undefined entities which merely appear and then vanish; the playwright's narrative offers a firm conclusion with the character of the disappearing passenger made plain – later events prove her to have been a *departed spirit*. Nonetheless, he would have had private personal satisfaction from meeting these fellow-witnesses of the Phantom Hitch-Hiker because, as he writes in conclusion:

I have often told this story, to people who are psychic, and given to dabble in the occult; and many and various are the explanations they have been offered. I have, however, always been able to give the one and only correct explanation – which is *that the thing never happened*. Still, as the White Knight said, *it's my own invention*.[6]

In plain language, Sutro made the story up; there isn't a grain of truth in it. Why he should have selected this particular theme for his 'psychic' improvisation is beside the point. Here is the essential paradox of the matter: the newspaper reports of vanishing hitch-hikers are presented as testimonies to fact, accounts of things that 'really happened'; yet the Phantom Hitch-Hiker is 24-carat folklore, or (less politely) fiction.

Assessing the credibility of the Hitch-Hiker

Are these stories true or not? We are accustomed to making a distinction between factual stories (incidents reported in our newspapers, for instance) and fictional ones (the eerie tales in volumes like *The Third Fontana Book of Great Ghost Stories*, to select a title at random). The Phantom Hitch-Hiker appears to belong in both or either category: it is allegedly true, but suspectedly false.

Setting aside their literal truth, or their specious approximation of it, these and other contemporaneous accounts illustrate the essential elements of the Hitch-Hiker motif. In each an ostensibly real hitch-hiker vanishes from a moving vehicle under conditions that patently indicate he or she was of apparitional origin – perhaps a departed spirit (ghost), but perhaps belonging to some other supernatural denomination (angel? demon? faery?). Note also the variations in secondary details. The Sassari and Peshawar cases typify two of the more common alternatives; in both instances the Hitch-Hiker climbs onto the pillion of a motor-cycle instead of occupying the passenger seat of a car and (more importantly) intelligent, detailed conversation passes between her and the witnesses. This latter characteristic is critical to the significance of the 'classical' Hitch-Hiker story, for as we will see, the conversation supplies vital evidence to corroborate the other-worldly nature of the incident.

Other variants are discernible. The Hitch-Hiker is capable of manifesting as male *or* female, but frequently takes the sex opposite to that of the driver – a factor which may excite the interest of psychoanalytically-orientated interpreters of the occult. Age and physical appearance vary from incident to incident: an old woman in black, a young girl in white, a man in his twenties, a thirty-to-forty-year-old male in a check jacket, and so on. Witnesses come singly or accompanied – two, three, four to a car. Apart from these individual touches the narrative line is not subject to much divergence, down to the noted reactions of the motorist-victims (great disbelief, shock, need for a drink) and of the police, who are generally reported to be taking the matter seriously. One oft-stated reason for their seriousness lies in the allegation that other drivers are said to have had identical (or similar) experiences at (or close to) the same spot: another point bearing on the popular assumption that the Hitch-Hiker is a ghost typically earthbound to the place where its physical life ended. Taken as a group, the individual variations within these Hitch-Hiker narratives do not disguise the obvious fact that we are dealing basically with the *same* story.

Alongside these thematic correspondences we have also found *contrasts*. The most notable of these relates to the way in which the stories conclude. The majority, like Alfred Sutro's, are neatly, artistically, tied up, leaving the reader in no doubt that the Hitch-Hiker *was* some kind of 'walking spirit'; but a handful end with the identity of the vanishing passenger unconfirmed – all we can say is that he/she cannot have been human, since humans lack the power to vanish from car seats after this fashion. Sutro's story firmly implies that the Hitch-Hiker was a ghost; those of Davidson-Acres and Fulton stop short of this implication yet defy us to find a rival explanation.

In all cases the Hitch-Hiker is described as a factual occurence – a stance either conveyed directly by the narrator or implicit in the fact the account appears in a medium concentrating exclusively upon factual occurrences (newspapers, books of authenticated instances of the paranormal). Sutro's delayed confession has a deflating effect; he tricks his readers by fabricating not just the story, but also the role of the 'trust-worthy narrator'. More to the point, he stimulates the suspicion that similar 'true' stories are equally bogus, even when reported as fact by national papers.

Parapsychologists have no choice but to confront this ambiguity. It is one thing to listen to and enjoy a ghost story told over a drink; it is quite another to assess its claims to be a genuine record of anomalous fact. And parapsychologists, of course, are bound to employ objective, scientific methodology. What criteria can be invoked to evaluate the Phantom Hitch-Hiker's credibility *outside* the folklore-fiction context in which it is normally understood to operate?

The opening gambit is surely to study and understand that context thoroughly: to view the ghost first in respect of its folklore heritage. By digesting the characteristics and conventions of the motif analyzed by various folklore authorities we will be able to see how each separate newspaper report conforms with or diverges from a body of material they classify as fiction-presented-as-fact. We may simultaneously ponder that 'open-ended' (inconclusive) ghost stories are not a popular form of folk-narrative, whereas psychical research features little else.

Folklore abounds with anonymous accounts in which the witness is merely designated by occupation (e.g., 'a doctor') or by personal relationship to the narrator ('a friend of a friend of mine'), and often by even less than these ('a man was driving home late at night . . .'). Can we improve on this by identifying a *named* witness – perhaps one whom investigators could contact and interview? Should this be the case (and presuming the witness does not emulate Alfred Sutro by springing a belated confession upon us!), how can we then substantiate his story? In most Phantom Hitch-Hiker episodes the witness is a solo motorist; he can provide no objective proof in support of his version of the event. This means a researcher is not merely contending with the problem of determining the witness's primary truthfulness. Even when satisfied that the witness is not fabricating the story, the investigator cannot be certain that the resulting account matches the facts of what actually transpired.

Chapter Four details some of the criteria by which investigators approach the problems of assessing the credibility of ghost stories told to them as facts; also, a few of the natural explanations – delusion, illusion, misidentification, malobservation – that must be considered *en route* to a paranormal interpretation of these incidents. Too often, though, the process is aborted at the very beginning. Phantom Hitch-Hiker witnesses are traditionally anonymous; even when a newspaper performs its usual function by naming the person featured in the story, it is likely that a researcher will nonetheless fail to trace and interview him. Hence we need to adopt an alternative line of inquiry.

The stories allege that the witnesses were sufficiently alarmed to bring their adventures to the attention of the authorities – the police or their equivalents – who respond in a manner to indicate that they accepted the reports as being worthy of following up. Again, folklore warns that in Hitch-Hiker stories police involvement is flourished as another pseudo-corroborative narrative element, one that enhances the credibility of an inherently incredible tale; by believing that the police took the thing seriously we are led to believe that the preceding part of the narrative was 'serious' (authentic) as well. Working from our newspaper data, can we find evidence that these elements – the Official Report, the Police Action and Statement – were genuine events that took place as described? In such a case we might conjecture that the story in hand contains a measure of validity: would persons approach the authorities with their flimsy ghost stories unless they honestly believed in what they were saying? Would the police pursue the issue even to the point of conceding bafflement if the initial report did *not* impress them as honestly rendered?

This book will suggest there *have* been cases featuring named witnesses, some of them subsequently interviewed by investigators who found no blatant evidence of fabrication. Confirmation is to be found of officially reported, officially pursued Hitch-Hiker incidents. What follows now is a foretaste of the problems and inferences arising both before and after a critical review of recently-gathered press accounts concerning this widely-dispersed phenomenon.

From classification to criticism

The Phantom Hitch-Hiker is a 'road-ghost' – meaning that it belongs to a broad tradition of ghost stories set on the open road. It would be convenient to separate the Hitch-Hiker from other motifs focusing upon transport-seeking apparitions like those said to materialize suddenly and without invitation in the backs of cars, as the 'old lady' seen by a Kendal taxi driver in 1974 was said to have done.[7] Unfortunately, such fine divisions are not consistently possible. Theoretically a well-defined concept, the Phantom Hitch-Hiker is likely to be found in combination with one or more disparate road-ghost themes.

For instance, there are widely-located stories of apparitions that habitually rush suddenly into the paths of oncoming traffic – or appear from nowhere directly in front of it – giving the drivers no chance to avoid collision with what they suppose to be real, destructible human pedestrians. The aftermath of this suicidal simulation is always the same: the driver halts in terror to look for a body and is considerably more terrified to find no trace of one.

A world of difference exists between these spectral jaywalkers and hitch-hikers who disappear from moving cars, yet not infrequently a road-ghost story cycle will incorporate both motifs. One of the more impressive incidents spoken of in connection with the ghostly girl reputed to haunt Blue Bell Hill, Kent, deals not with her conventional hitch-hiking penchant, but the assumption that she is synonymous with the small child run over by bricklayer Maurice Goodenough in 1974. This episode will receive closer attention in a later chapter; suffice it to say for the moment that in the interim between Mr Goodenough wrapping the bleeding child in a blanket and the arrival of the police, the stricken body somehow absented itself from the scene – leaving no blood traces and not even enough scent for a tracker dog to follow.

This involvement of the police, tracker dogs and all, serves as a reminder that not everyone accepts the Phantom Hitch-Hiker purely as a creature of folklore. The very action of calling in the authorities (just as would be appropriate in a mundane motoring misadventure) argues that a few people feel the opposite. Like Maurice Goodenough before him, Roy Fulton took the trouble to notify the police of an experience that objective common sense might have assured him could not happen outside the pages of fiction. But he was *not* claiming to be in a position where common sense applied; with some justification, perhaps, he might have borrowed the quotation resorted to by Sir William Crookes when replying to criticisms of his experiments with the medium D. D. Home: 'I never said it was possible, I only said it was true.'[8]

Such a stance is either the mark of a notably brazen hoaxer or of someone who at least believes he is stating the truth, regardless of any 'normal explanation' the experts may later attach to his experience. As Inspector Rowland of Dunstable commented, the police 'hear strange things from people'. That these sometimes assault the officers' incredulity as forcibly as that of the witnesses can be allowed; that occasionally the person offering the story may be mentally disturbed (a 'crazy') can also be accepted. Yet somewhere along the line and despite his imitation of rationality, the 'crazy' almost always gives a clue that reveals him to be a largely harmless if unbalanced attention seeker. Roy Fulton and Maurice Goodenough, it would appear, did not strike the authorities in this way: to all

Two modestly-sized hills in southern England share the same Hitch-Hiker haunted reputation: Blue Bell Hill (above), Kent, and Gibbet Hill (below), on the Frome-Nunney road in Somerset. (*author's photographs*)

intents and purposes they were ordinary, sober people caught up in what they believed was a bizarre but actual event.

Prompt reporting increases a story's credibility-quotient even more, as B. Dupi observed when summarizing a Phantom Hitch-Hiker episode for the French magazine *Lumieres dans la Nuit*.[9] Close to midnight on 20 May 1981 a mature woman in a white mackintosh and headscarf hitched a ride at the Quatre Canaux bridge just outside Palavas-les-Flots, a seaside resort near Montpellier. Her arrival forced a seating rearrangement on the four occupants of the red two-door Renault 5: she ended by sitting between two girls in the rear of the car. Some 200 metres before Pont Vert the Hitch-Hiker drowned the music from the cassette radio with a cry of, 'Mind the bend. You are risking your life!'. The vehicle duly slowed down, the bend was negotiated safely, and the passengers abruptly realized that their number had been reduced from five back to the original four. The woman in white had vanished.

The quartet went straightway to the main police station in Montpellier where Inspector Lopez tactfully advised them that if their story was a hoax there was still time to come clean about it – no punitive action would be taken. But, he informed researchers afterwards, "their panic wasn't put on and we soon realized they were genuine. It worried us"'. Following a fruitless investigation of the incident-scene, police and witnesses retired once more to the station where statements were formally taken – matching statements, as it happened.

The Montpellier Hitch-Hiker must be viewed in perspective – against a collection of virtually identical stories current throughout France and Spain over the previous five years. In most of these the 'autostoppeuse' cautioned drivers about bends where fatal crashes had occured (sometimes adding darkly, 'I know all about it') and vanished once the car had come safely through the hazard. These admonitory car-travelling ghosts also revealed for local investigators a less comforting pattern: in all cases the witnesses were anonymous or 'had left the area', and in at least one (Sanlucar la Mayor, Seville, September 1977) the story was exposed as a definite fable – causing the writer to acidly remark on 'a tissue of lies [*fabrication de canulars*] circulating in France and Spain'.[10]

In the Palavas-les-Flots affair, though, we have four witnesses (albeit designated only by forenames) convincing a police officer of their sincerity; an officer who was evidently alive to the possibilty of a hoax and who gave them the opportunity to retract without risk to themselves. In the final analysis a reader is left with the possibility of the quartet – perhaps concertedly using a story of recent currency as their model – brazening out the charade, *or* alternatively the possibility that they honestly believed in their Hitch-Hiker adventure . . .

Still skirting the issue of whether or not all these witnesses were ambitious liars or honest people – even deluded-but-honest people – we can move our attention to a small corner of Somerset where once again local police have received ostensibly *bona fide* reports from distressed motorist-victims of a Phantom Hitch-Hiker. In 1977 the villagers of Nunney were said to be out in force to trap a ghost that was jeopardizing the prospects of their Silver Jubilee festivities. It also constituted a formidable safety hazard: one man claimed that the sight of the figure – standing in the middle of the road at or about the same point from which he'd hitched a ride with the unsuspecting motorist some time before (only to vanish *en route* after the usual fashion) – had been the reason he had slewed his car into a lamp-post. When people began to avoid Nunney Lane, a narrow thorough-fare leading from the village to Frome, nearly three miles away, it seemed to bode ill to the hopes that visitors would be lured by the Jubilee celebrations and a group of residents under the leadership of a building society manager decided to lay the inauspicious spirit.

Newspaper summaries of how they set about this demanding task made intentionally comic reading. We are told that the group, including representatives from the parish council and local government, took noise detectors, tape recorders, light meters and what was described as a 'ghost catching net' and that they climbed trees and scrambled through hedges in a vain endeavour to come to grips with the mystery. The idea of netting a ghost revives Charles Fort's thoughtful words on a roughly comparable situation at Euroa when (it was said) Melbourne Zoological Gardens despatched someone equipped in a similar manner to investigate reports of a 30-foot monster: 'the man with a net is a significant character. He had not the remotest of ideas of using it, but, just the same, he went along with it'.[11]

The Nunney ghost-net may have been writers' copy based on something more functional, but in any eventuality its carrier had no more chance to enmesh an anomaly than did his counterpart from Melbourne Zoo on the Euroa monster-hunt. Still, the earnestness of the vigilantes made undeniably good material for a human interest story. What will you actually do, asked one journalist, if the ghost appears? The reply: '"I suppose we'd have to reason with him"'. Not long afterwards the practical jokers moved in and a ghoulish face painted on a white sheet suspended over the road robbed the apparition of much of its credibility.[12]

However humorous press reports of the Nunney ghost-patrols were made to sound, they undoubtedly served a neo-serious purpose. Readers were encouraged to remember that such outlandish behaviour on the part of otherwise sane individuals was inspired by *genuine* fear of a *genuine* ghost. In this way the papers used the nocturnal hunts as evidence that people in this part of the world believed in the Phantom Hitch-Hiker; by extension, therefore, the ghost had to possess some factual basis.

Folklore and beyond

The failure of the Nunney vigilantes to net the enigma was not surprising. It is a truly rare occasion when a ghost will manifest on cue. Moreover, these manifestations can seldom be traced to an indisputably real historical cause. One of the most annoying contrasts that parapsychologists face when involved with cases of this type is the gulf between the apparently motiveless apparition, whose *raison d'être* is undetectable, and the 'fact' that traditionally such phantoms are always equipped with meaning, motive and purpose. To put it another way, the psychical researcher is confronted by a ghost that simply appears and vanishes, while the popular belief is in ghosts who 'walk' for more or less logical reasons: they are conveyors of warnings or other important information to the living, terrorisers of criminals guilty of as-yet undisclosed crimes, souls condemned to atone for misdeeds, and so on.

Sutro's ghost-girl was the spirit of a tragically-drowned child and had ample reason to haunt the scene of her death; the Stanbridge, Nunney and other presumed Phantom Hitch-Hikers showed no just cause for being where they were or for doing what they did. These old, cherished beliefs add a measure of logic to the illogical world of ghosts. Faced by repeated events of the haunting type, it is not strange that people should attempt, with varying degrees of seriousness, to assign the apparition meaning, motive and rationale, rather than let it pass into obscurity as a random event. The most common motif put forward in Phantom Hitch-Hiker narratives is based firmly on this kind of 'logical' explanation. Quite simply, as in Sutro's 'own invention', the apparition is a spirit, a former victim of tragic, accidental death.

This motif not only holds out certain attractions for those who believe Phantom Hitch-Hikers should possess comprehensible reasons for what they do: in many instances it is crucial to the entire fabric of the story. Typically, the Peshawar Hitch-Hiker was attributed to the spirit of a girl killed by a truck as she waited for her boyfriend; Chicago's 'Resurrection Mary', named after the cemetery in which she was buried after being mowed down by a car, is supposedly still trying to complete the journey back home that she started sometime in the 1930s.[13] Similarly unspecified vehicles are believed to have accounted for the originals of the London-Worthing Road Hitch-Hiker and another incessantly-weeping girl purportedly picked up by three couples inside a week near Southampton.[14] The more persistent hauntings of Blue Bell Hill have at various times been speculatively traced to the deaths of *either* four girls (a bride-to-be and her three attendants) in 1965 *or* to two girls killed in a car crash in 1967.[15]

While intended to add credibility to a story, these conjectural endings have an opposite, adverse effect. By drawing the accounts into line with those familiar from folklore treatments of the supernatural they make it easy assume they *are* folklore – that is, fiction. A sceptic may ignore such details as the extreme unlikelihood of a girl hitch-hiker handing out her name, address and sometimes even her telephone number to the complete stranger who has picked her up; this, we now understand, is a narrative device essential if the 'witness' is to establish her identity with a deceased person. But he will seize upon the fact that the proposed historical motivation behind the haunting – the tragic road accident – is almost always founded on no actual evidence. It there *was* no tragic accident, he reasons, there could have been no ghost; therefore the allegedly-authentic Hitch-Hiker must be a fabrication.

Already we have noticed that certain reports – those of Roy Fulton and Cedric Davidson-Acres – omit any sort of explanatory ending. Admittedly, these are poorly constructed tales from an artistic viewpoint, but they are closer to the inconclusive kind of accounts common throughout parapsychology – accounts submitted to scientific interrogation and held to be factual. The indication is that, for want of an artificial ending or on behavioural grounds, these ghosts which merely appear and then vanish without hint of identity or purpose might also belong to parapsychological fact rather than to folklore's fiction. This first impresssion ought to provide a valid justification for examining cases like Stanbridge and Jambataan Merdeka more closely. Perhaps there will be cogent internal clues to support this prior assumption.

Implications and meanings

There are further justifications for a serious, multi-directional survey of the Phantom Hitch-Hiker. '"If there's no meaning in it,"' as the King of Hearts said of a certain set of verses, '"that saves a world of trouble, you know, as we needn't try to find any. And yet I don't know . . . I seem to see some meaning in them after all."'[16] So too with Hitch-Hiker tales.

The Phantom Hitch-Hiker being just another form of ghost story, it can be treated in the same way as other branches of the art. For the vast majority of us, ghost stories are not inbued with genuine significance: they are simply an accepted form of undemanding entertainment. The genre, an uneasy blend of fact and fiction so combined as to be almost indistinguishable, has been around too long for us to take the implications of individual components like the Phantom Hitch-Hiker seriously.

In truth, it is the *sensation* rather than the implication that really attracts us. On the whole, ghost stories (true ones, fictional ones or the intermediate variety) do not alter our conceptions of life, the universe or anything else. Those propagated by newspapers are fundamentally ephemeral and forgettable. What tends to survive in the mind of the average reader is not the specifics – names, locations – but the generalities; perhaps these are reduced to a dim recollection of a hitch-hiker who vanished from a moving car, a ghost by inference. The possibilty that such detritus may hover in the memory for a far greater length of time, and with dynamic results, constitutes a major theme of latter parts of this text.

The essence of telling a successful ghost story, whether orally or in writing, is to present it as a stone-cold *fact*. Regardless of how incredible it may seem, how remote from probability are the events with which it deals, the tale must come across as a seriously-narrated item, one that will challenge but not insult the hearers'/readers' sense of what is or is not possible. The Victorian writers who accrued such high reputations as purveyors of weird tales and their 'True Accounts' of hauntings that were purely the products of their imaginations relied heavily on this understanding of what is proper to the ghost story; sometimes so successfully that we are never certain that every part of what they write is *solely* the product of that imagination. To take just one example, Le Fanu's 'Authentic Narrative of a Haunted House' is not far removed from the kind of eye-witness record presented in the early issues of the *Proceedings* of the Society for Psychical Research, which printed nothing but the most strongly-evidenced cases. Thanks to its peculiarly reserved mode of telling it drifts in a region that could be either fact *or* fiction.[17]

The ghosts of folklore are also hybrids of fact and fiction and so long as the stories in which they appear are good ones, most people are not concerned about proof of their literal reality. The Phantom Hitch-Hiker is a folklore ghost *par excellence* – a story told so often as 'fact' that no one actually interested in solid evidence will ever believe it is anything other than fiction. Folklore does not primarily concern itself with corroborative details like names of witnesses, dates and places, and the stories are not subjected to the quasi-legalistic process by which parapsychologists evaluate ghostly matters.

Hence there is every reason for being suspicious about the Phantom Hitch-Hiker, even when he/she/it appears in what we are encouraged to believe is 100 per cent truthful newspaper reportage. We have been conditioned to take the 'truth guarantee' at face value and to settle back to enjoy (then forget) what follows. Why worry about whether the ghost has a message or a meaning?

As the King of Hearts mused: '"And yet I don't know . . . I seem to see some meaning in [it] after all"'. The occurrence of the same story with only minor thematic variations over such a wide area of the world suggests that the Hitch-Hiker is a highly popular ghost – perhaps even a loved one – for all its repetitious behaviour. How can this be, unless the story touches some deep core within the narrators, the listeners, the readers? Can it be that ghost stories are more important to us than we think?

Even more intriguing: in a small fraction of these stories there is firm evidence that people have approached an official body (the police) to report an experience which simultaneously meets all the criteria by which they themselves judge actual, real-life events. And where ghost stories are concerned, a small fraction can be a very significant one . . .

A story, or a story come to life?

Time and again the Phantom Hitch-Hiker is being presented as a fact – but it need not necessarily be a fact at all.

Even if it is *not*, the story deserves better than to be consigned to oblivion. A more rewarding approach would be to set down a number of modestly-proposed questions designed to explore the dynamics of this persistent motif, such as:

– If the Phantom Hitch-Hiker is no more than just another ghost story, why is it so widely spread and (equally curious) so durable? There are many other more dramatic ghost stories, tales far more memorable and exciting, which have *not* survived.

The death-pact apparition who testifies to its reality by leaving the mark of its burning grasp on the witness's wrist has become a grand piece of spectral archaism, seldom heard of nowadays; by contrast the Hitch-Hiker is still on the road and its range is practically global. If it is just another story, what is so remarkable about it that we refuse to let it die?

The implication of the survival-qualities of this well-worn, foot-weary phantom might therefore suggest that some aspects of folklore are more subtle, more important, than we give them credit for being in this highly streamlined age of ours. Following from this:

– Does the story hold some special significance for us? Does it convey or reflect some particular aspiration? Today we look to the television and to disaster-horror films for our sensations. Does the Phantom Hitch-Hiker motif, seemingly so tame and contrived in comparison with these slickly-devised terrors, fulfil some folk-art role, perhaps conforming to our notions of how and why hauntings are performed?

It is too easy to dismiss a ghost story simply because one has heard it before – or because it is fashionable to be cynical about anything the newspapers choose to print. Whatever our suspicions about the authenticity of each tale, we must look at it carefully in its own right before we consign it to the rubbish-heap.

– Is there *any* evidence that *any* of these vanishing Hitch-Hiker accounts might be true? Rephrasing this, how trustworthy are journalistic descriptions of these alleged events; and at the next stage removed, how trustworthy are the witnesses themselves? If on both levels the narrators are lying (or to be charitable, indulging in creative urges to fabricate), why are the same old lies-fabrications being told?

As Andrew Lang wrote:

Even ghost stories . . . have some basis of fact, whether fact of hallucination, or illusion, or imposture. They are, at lowest, 'human documents'.[18]

Basis of fact, human documents. Ghost stories are, one way or another, strange fragments of human experience, attested to by our fellow-men and women. They reveal to us something about the way in which we function; they invite us to theorize, to probe our limited understanding. Once we look beyond the sensational side of ghost stories deeper levels become apparent.

The presence of the Phantom Hitch-Hiker around our car-inhabited globe implies that the story must have *some* meaning,

Andrew Lang (1844-1912), one of the most talented and versatile writers of his day, had an especial interest in ghost stories. 'They are,' he wrote, 'at lowest, human documents.' (*National Portrait Gallery, London*)

some significance. Andrew Lang lived in the days when motorized transport was still something of a novelty – not that this indicates that the Hitch-Hiker can only travel when and where there are automobiles; there is evidence that he/she is far older than the car. But Lang, who knew all about the durability of ghost stories, made a comment that is highly relevant to the motif. Of another recurring narrative he said:

The story . . . is clearly one of the tales which come round in cycles, either because events repeat themselves or because people will unconsciously localize old legends in new places and assign old occurrences or fables to new persons.[19]

Regardless of how many times the Phantom Hitch-Hiker is presented as fact, there will be little resistance from researchers to the evidence that most stories featuring the itinerant ghost are fabricated, folklore creations retold in new settings. The next chapter underscores this and offers the ostensible ubiquity of the Hitch-Hiker as testimony to the fluid nature and potency of old folk-traditions in our modern age where, at first sight, they are anachronisms. It is no small thing that we are still telling these 'creepy stories' – and in the same old manner, as if they were true events that happened to ourselves or our acquaintances. But there is more to it than this.

Lang suggests that, where ghosts are concerned, events may repeat themselves. The existence of a doubtfully-attested or admittedly-fictional body of vanishing Hitch-Hiker stories has convinced all but a handful of researchers that there is no literal truth behind any of them; but surely before supporting such a conclusion we must look at the evidence. It may be that the sceptics are right and that there is *no* evidence that anyone has ever acted as chauffeur for a Phantom Hitch-Hiker. On the other side of the coin, if there *is* evidence, then we are not dealing with make-believe only. The inference would be that these motorists' stories represent a specific kind of paranormal phenomenon – and the Phantom Hitch-Hiker might consequently be the concern of parapsychology as well as of folklore. Should that prove so, researchers would be advised to reassess their approach to the business of ghosts and ghosts-seeing – not least of all, to redefine what constitutes acceptable evidence in spontaneous cases.

It is a sound maxim that remarkable (paranormal) events can only be accepted upon remarkably *strong* evidence. The Phantom Hitch-Hiker challenges our resolution on this issue. Credible-seeming people are testifying to incredible experiences. Do we reject their stories because they cannot be supported by independent testimony – because the motorist involved was on his own at the time he alleges he picked up the Hitch-Hiker? The sensible reaction is to agree that we *should* reject the stories on these grounds. But elsewhere investigators have been swayed by the credibility of solo witnesses into waiving this right of veto. And what of cases like Palavas-les-Flots where *four* witnesses agree to having experienced the same fantastical-sounding adventure? These incidents may be collectively-told lies rather than collective sightings, yet, as before, the researcher has a duty to *prove* the allegation instead of promoting it for the want of a better idea.

I said earlier that the Phantom Hitch-Hiker conformed to a well-established pattern: the ghost story as a source of entertainment. It remains to be asked why a series with such a threadbare script is still running. We can start on reasonably firm ground – the folklorist's home ground – by considering how widely spread the story of the Phantom Hitch-Hiker is and to what initial conclusions its levels of distribution may lead us.

TWO: THE VANISHING HITCHHIKER
a much-travelled story

The ubiquity of poltergeist incidents – the fact that showers of stones, for example, have been reported all over the world regardless of the passage of history and of cultural, social or educational deviations between the races observing them – has struck more than one parapsychologist as a cogent argument for the reality of the phenomena. Yet strangely enough, it is not thought legitimate to extend this collectivist approach towards apparitions. The theory works well enough up to the point where we agree that, because so many people have seen phantoms, the experience of ghost-seeing (though presently inexplicable) bears a certain credibilty; but the repeated accounts featuring *specific* types of apparition – ghostly highwaymen, peripatetic Anne Boleyns, assorted Ladies in Grey or Black, *and* of course Phantom Hitch-Hikers – do not help persuade the sceptically-inclined that they 'exist'. Paradoxically, reports of this kind have the opposite effect. Confronted by so many near-identical tales of vanishing passengers, the perceptive critic will point out that the story in question is of respectable vintage and that it appears to have been kicked about from one locality to another: that it is not really the property of parapsychology, but of folklore.

Finding in Stith Thompson's index of folklore motifs an individual entry reading: 'E332.1.1. The Vanishing Hitch-Hiker' raises the expectation that folklorists are well-accustomed to variations on this theme and that they have devised ways in which to render them logical. So indeed it proves: so indeed they have.

The Hitch-Hiker dissected

Look, for instance, at Ernest W. Baughman's monumental work, the *Type-and Motif-Index of the Folk Tales of England and North America*.[1] Here, in two pages, we have the Phantom Hitch-Hiker and his/her confederate spirits in graded order, neatly classified and defined in terms of their essential behaviour. Passing through various entries for assorted transport-seeking apparitions, the reader comes to:

The Vanishing Hitchhiker. Ghost of young woman asks for ride in automobile, disappears from closed car without the driver's knowledge, after giving him an address to which she wishes to be taken. The driver asks person at the address about the rider, finds she has been dead for some time. (Often the driver finds that the ghost has made similar attempts to return, usually on anniversary of death in automobile accident. Often, too, the ghost leaves some item such as a scarf or a travelling bag in the car.)

This is entry E332.3.3.1. Almost every facet of the ghost's performance merits a separate classification number. The anniversary-active Hitch-Hiker is E332.3.3.1 (a); the item-leaver 3.3.1 (b); while if the item happens to be a pool of water deposited by the recently-drowned girl, as in one story from Waikiki, that makes it an E332.3.3.1 (c). Old ladies who vanish after uttering doom-laden prophecies of disaster, war and the downfall of great cities are lumped together under 3.3.1 (d), with the next three categories representing phantoms sufficiently corporeal as to indulge in eating, drinking and even love-making with the motorist (.3.1e), those who want to be taken to their dying sons (3.1f) or simply to be taken home (3.1g). A surprisingly large grouping of vanishing nuns also appears (.3.1h, 3.1i, 3.1j), some of whom are also prophetic. Lastly there are deities who take to the road as hitch-hikers (E332.3.3.2), one of the most persistent being the Hawaiian goddess Pele or Pelee (3.2a).

As an example of how the material can be analysed the Baughman Index is invaluable, but it has still more to offer in the form of abbreviated references to relevant articles and papers on the topic in hand. Reading through the entries under the headings just summarized, two names become familiar. They belong to Richard K. Beardsley and Rosalie Hankey, who in 1942/43 contributed two of the most exhaustive and important studies on the folklore of Phantom Hitch-Hikers that have ever been published. In fact, no one with any interest in this, the 'most popular of the current ghost tales in America', as another authority has described it,[2] can afford to ignore the two issues of the *California Folklore Quarterly* which contain their joint efforts.[3] Seeing how many later writers have adopted Beardsley and Hankey's system, assigning each freshly-retrieved Phantom Hitch-Hiker to one or more of the four variants detected by this industrious couple, there follows a short condensation of their findings. In particular these deserve to be known more widely among researchers in that nebulously-connected discipline, parapsychology.

A Beardsley and Hankey digest

Inspired by a fairly typical San Fransciscan Phantom Hitch-Hiker story from a businessman – a friend, it seemed, of the writers' informant – Beardsley and Hankey set about collecting as many variations and analogues as possible. Within two months oral and postal sources had supplied them with over 60 specimens, more than enough to support their premise that 'the legend was told all over the United States'.[4] Adding to their final total of 79 stories – 40 of which were reproduced in their first paper – the 49 others cited by Louis C. Jones as part of the New York State College Folklore Archives, the statement can hardly be disputed, though the noun 'legend' might be. Within this impressive gathering of roadside revenants the authors identified 'four distinctly different versions, distinguishable because of obvious differences in development and essence'.[5] Labelled alphabetically, these are:

Stories where the Hitch-Hiker gives an address, through which the motorist learns he has just given a lift to a ghost . . .

Version A

Stories where the Hitch-Hiker is an old woman who prophesies disaster or at the end of World War II; subsequent inquiries likewise reveal her to be deceased . . .

Version B

Stories where a girl is met at some place of entertainment, e.g., a dance, instead of on the road; she leaves some token (often the overcoat she borrowed from the motorist) on her grave by way of corroborating the experience and her identity . . .

Version C

Stories where the Hitch-Hiker is later identified as a local deity . . .

Version D

In their subsequent paper Beardsley and Hankey concluded that Version A, derived from some undiscovered source, was closest to what they surmised to be the 'original' story, containing as it did the seminal elements of the motif. Versions B and D apeared to them local derivants of A (with additional, specialized details), as C might also have been despite a wider distribution. The writers suggested that the C variant had formerly started life as a completely different ghostly tale (with elements nonetheless common to A and B) which at some stage was converted into a Phantom Hitch-Hiker story.

Some 49 per cent of Beardsley and Hankey's sample came into the Version A category – the most widely-distributed of the four variants, represented in sixteen states of the USA (including New York, California, Texas and Hawaii), as well as in Mexico, which yielded a single, prolonged and decidedly bizarre instance of the genre. As might be expected, the crucial episode in any Version A story is the revelation of the girl's non-human status, which contrasts with the reigning normality in the preceding portion of the tale. The B stories are categorically different: all save one of the nine examples are centred on Chicago and its environs and, more noteworthy, the young girl is replaced by an old woman with the supernatural character of the Hitcher largely subservient to the element of prophecy, which the disappearance of the passenger actually reinforces.

The date of the end of the Second World War is the sort of thing upon which the hitch-hiking nuns concentrate in Beardsley and Hankey stories from San Francisco and Chicago, both of them current around 1941/42, and seven more were disclosed by Professor Jones' survey to display a lively interest in the same matter. He adds that one of these, widely talked of in the autumn of 1941 among the people of Kingston, New York, was later identified as Mother Cabrini, founder of the Sacred Heart Orphanage, who was beatified for her good works. In this instance the 'B' nun was evidently on her way to acquiring 'D' status – the Hitch-Hiker as local divinity – and the broad circulation of the story is testified to by the fact that the clergy had reputedly felt moved to issue an official repudiation of it.[6]

Not all the B Version women are interested in world wars. Commensurate with the argument that this variant was born in Chicago around 1933, two at least prophesy disaster at the Century of Progress Exposition, or (shades of an old local legend concerning the slide of the Windy City into Lake Michigan, think Beardsley and Hankey) that Northerly Island will be submerged. Another, from Waukesha, Wisconsin, foresees trouble at the World's Fair, while a large but unnamed Midwest city is the venue for an epidemic in the opinion of another equally lugubrious passenger. The strict topicality of these Hitch-Hikers' choices of conversation or prophecy ought to have spelled rapid obsolescence for the motif – but such certainly was not the case.

Prophetic Hitch-Hikers of the 1970s

Far from being tied to time (the 1940s) and place (the American Midwest) these prophets of the open road appear to have kept on travelling. Some three decades later, and far from Chicago, a typical instance was reported near the Austro-German border, where the Hitch-Hiker confronted a 43-year-old businessman at Greifnau. Although favouring nun-like garb, her behaviour sounds distinctly unreligious: taking a seat next to the driver (who responded out of the goodness of his heart to her request for a lift at around midnight), the weird old lady refused to answer his questions and muttered sourly about some imminent evil that *The News of the World* report of 13 April 1975 does not expand upon. The rest of the story more or less follows the recognized formula: the woman vanished, causing the unlucky motorist so much alarm that he nearly crashed into an approaching vehicle: other drivers claim comparable adventures, though in some the woman disappears even before getting into the car, or merely sits in silence before dematerializing. Still in keeping with the story's usual development, the police are said to be taking the matter seriously – the local chief has threatened anyone who spreads the story farther with a £200 fine, since a species of panic has gripped the area, with parents keeping their children off the haunted road both by night and by day. Also 'taking it seriously': a group of Austrian psychical researchers who, perhaps impressed by the allegation that an amateur photographer has taken a picture of a shadowy figure, conveyed electronic devices and high-speed cameras across the border in the hope of probing the enigma. Whether they did so or not is left unanswered; at this point the article ends.

Here is a story presented as fact, but within the folklore mould – a Version B Hitch-Hiker with a somewhat ambiguous prophetic element. This factor is better developed in a February 1977 example set in Northern Italy. Steve Moore's résumé of this case combines material from *La Stampa* of 25/26 February and 1 March, *Stampa Sera*, 28 February, and even the *Dallas Morning News*, 25 February, for that year:[7] these sources stated that several motorists admitted to have given rides to an old woman who prophesied the destruction of Milan by earthquake on the 27th of the month. Of course she vanished, leaving some form of evidence that she had died ten years previously (like the Catholic nun from Chicago in Beardsley and Hankey's 18th story). Also true to type is the denouement: for all its supernaturally-invested trappings, the prediction was not fulfilled and the manic fascination of thousands of Italians ended when the old city remained unscathed by seismic disaster. Steve Moore adds that the North Italian panic-reaction to the rumours was not completely unintelligible in the light of the previous year's catastrophes following the ominous failure of St Janarius's preserved blood to liquify on cue.

Still in the grand apocalyptic manner, near Little Rock, Arkansas three years later another 'highway apostle' – a well-dressed, presentable young man – was known from a couple of incidents reported to the police as well as from rumours. This traveller proclaimed the Second Coming of Christ before he vanished; one newspaper noted that he also discussed less momentous current affairs, such as the holding of the hostages at the American Embassy in Iran.[8] State Trooper Robert Roten, who appears to have been the source of most of this information, commented that although hitch-hiking was illegal in the area, the prophet's tendency towards disappearance posed problems for arresting officers.

Equally interesting is the fact that he could only trace *two* logged reports of this type – two officially notified to the police, in contrast with the glut of verbal versions familiar to Little Rockers at third-hand or even more. According to the *Little Rock Gazette* of 25 July 1980, the first of these came from a female witness – it is not clear whether or not the police recorded her name – who claimed to have met the Hitch-Hiker on Highway 65 near Conway the preceding month (29 June); he talked of 'how bad things were' before vanishing. The following Sunday (6 July) a man who insisted on remaining anonymous gave the authorities a secondhand account of a group sighting between Little Rock and Benton in which the Hitch-Hiker's prophecy was more meteorological in character – announcing it would never rain again, he promptly relieved the startled motorists of his company. In one form or another this story was well known throughout the state – and beyond – but in none of the numerous newspaper columns devoted to it does there appear the name of an actual witness who testifies to it as *his* or *her* direct experience.[9]

The *Sunday People*'s correspondent in New York added a fresh but confusing dimension. Contemporary with the strange events at Little Rock came a series of incidents in Oregon, where a 50-to-60 year-old woman in a nun's habit was said to be hitching rides, talking about God and salvation and then vanishing – sometimes when the car involved was travelling at quite a speed. One witness had, moreover, been adjured to repent his sins – if he did not, he was scheduled to die in an accident.[10]

The New York correspondent was only describing the tip of the iceberg. Some of the many reports dealing with this elderly lady – dressed either as a nun or else 'expensively' – who frequented stretches of Interstate 5 between Tacoma, Washington, and Eugene, Oregon, noted a certain concern she displayed for the now notorious Mount St Helens. The *Midnight Globe* of 5 August 1980, quoting two police officers *and* one witness from a cast of dozens, stated that she told a driver that the May eruption of this volcano had signified God's warning to the people of the North-West and that those who did not return to Him could expect to perish in the Mount's next eruption, the liklihood of which occurrence experts were still trying to assess. The dynamics of this, the strangest of modern Hitch-Hiker story-complexes, take us well beyond the Chicagoan prophetic nuns observed by Beardsley and Hankey: so much so that full exploration of the mythos will be left until the final stages of this present book.

More variations on the theme

Beardsley and Hankey's Version C Hitch-Hiker is always a young girl, encountered only in dance halls, bars and other places of amusement (though Jones found three New York examples where she preferred the more conventional roadside ambiance). She does not vanish as such; she simply leaves the car at her destination – her former home, or even better, the cemetery – taking with her some borrowed item of the motorist-hero's clothing which she will drape over her grave as confirmation that the incident was not merely a dream and of her true identity. Often this token is the driver's overcoat.[11] Jones thinks that the unnatural coldness of which the girl complains (the chill of the grave, we are intended to assume?) can be seen as both a clue to her ghostly nature *and* a device whereby it becomes logical for her to borrow such a garment.

Louis C. Jones found not only overcoats on graves; at these macabre locations he also discovered the ultimate proof-item, namely a photograph connecting the Hitch-Hiker with an indisputably deceased individual. The photograph submotif, he notes, is not unique to the two Version C and three Version B stories in his New York collection, for it also appears in at least two of Italo-and Irish-American tales wholly unrelated to Phantom Hitch-Hikers. Both forms of corroboration appear together in a short news report from the *Sunday People* of 11 March 1973 – which, it may be worth recalling, prints it as sober fact.[12]

'Luigi takes a ghostly ride' deals with matters that would have been run-of-the-mill to Beardsley, Hankey and Jones. Motor cyclist Luigi Torres of Sassari, Sicily, lends his overcoat to a female pillion-rider and finds it next day on the ground close to the grave of a girl who died tragically three years before. As if further proof were needed, a photograph *above* the grave confirms beyond all doubt that Lucia Galante, deceased at only nineteen years of age, was one and the same as the hitch-hiker of the previous evening.[13] Or proof, a cynic might say, that you can't believe all you read in the newspapers.

One might as well believe in Laurie, heroine of a saccharine little ballad released back in the 1960s when ghostly girls were spasmodically made the subject of pop songs. Laurie emerges as a Phantom Hitch-Hiker who does not get a lift; instead she allows the nice boy singing the song to walk her home and trips indoors wearing the sweater he lent her when 'she said that she was very, very cold'. Of course this ends up on her grave – though not before the singer has been prepared for the worst by the dead girl's father. As we might have guessed, the 'incident' marks the anniversary of her demise.

The song has a recurrent refrain to the effect that strange things happen in the world, and indeed they do. On a more prosaic level, though, 'Laurie' is a fine example of an old theme given new currency; even the replacement of an overcoat with a sweater as proof-item is no accident. At the time the record was released,[14] stylish sweaters were a vital article in the average teenage trendsetter's wardrobe. This reworking of a small detail for the benefit of specific audiences (here, adolescent record-buyers) is a typical feature of folk-narratives, not least of the Phantom Hitch-Hiker story.

Version Cs are imbued with what might loosely be called a more 'literary' atmosphere than the other three variants. This means the basic narrative creaks with artifice; Beardsley and Hankey reflect that the return-to-the-grave introduces a hint of malevolence, or perhaps a vampiristic motif, enhanced by the occasional feature where the motorist goes insane or dies as a result of the encounter. There are eight typical Version Cs in the Beardsley and Hankey sample. The stylizations, though found in older, non-American ghostlore – the cemetery setting, the unnatural lightness or chill of the girl and the ethereal quality of her movements, for instance –[15] are not typical of the Phantom Hitch-Hiker canon overall and the authors hypothesize that they may owe a debt to the horror films released by Universal in the 1930s. Professor Jones agrees that Frankenstein, Dracula and his Daughter may have influenced the development of this version; he finds it 'more dramatic, and as such perhaps more literary than the general run of stories in Version A'.[16]

Hawaii, where the authors also found two Version As, plus some variations upon the same motif, is the proper home of the last major adaption of the Vanishing Hitchhiker. But Version D contains no ghost: Pele is a veritable goddess, whose appearance (according to other authorities) is believed to foreshadow the eruption of Mauna Loa, on whose slopes she can be found. Although no such disaster followed in the tales discovered by Beardsley and Hankey, another aspect of the Pele myth was mentioned: it is considered bad luck (or worse) not to offer her a lift when she is encountered. For this reason two negligent motorists in an undated story from Oahu retraced their journey to where they had passed an old basket-carrying woman who had mysteriously vanished soon after they overtook her; the drivers reasoned that they may have given offence by passing what could only have been the local divinity. Finally, Beardsley and Hankey round off their paper with twenty-three more variants on the Hitch-Hiker theme.

The detailed studies of Beardsley and Hankey have had a sustained impact on the relatively well-circumscribed area of folklore occupied by the Phantom Hitch-Hiker. As well as the work of Louis C. Jones, already cited, there have been numerous contributions which help to set this roadside wraith into its folklore context, many of them dating from the 1970s when there was a resurgence of 'true-life' accounts of Phantom Hitch-Hikers throughout the world. Some of these valuable sources will be alluded to later: for the moment we need to reflect on what such an abundance of material might indicate.

The immediate, inescapable conclusion is that we are dealing with a motif so broadly distributed that it is seemingly impossible to regard it as anything other than folk-fiction. An optimist may argue that perhaps at some remote point in time a factual incident along the lines of the Version A story actually took place and became the legitimate prey of narrators everywhere, with modification, relocation and improvisation occuring after the fashion common to good tales – ghostly or otherwise – the world over. But the conjecture is not likely to overpower the received opinion that the Phantom Hitch-Hiker is solidly folklore.

This assumption poses some problems. When Jacqueline Simpson was handed a 'classic' Hitch-Hiker story by an oral informant back in 1971 – complete with parents who told the motorist that the girl he described was their daughter, run over three years since while trying to hitch a lift outside the

Horsham café where she had vanished from his sight – the listener understandably treated the tale as part of the rich folklore tradition.[17] The folklorist was doubtless right in doing so; the story has all the hallmarks of artificiality. Nonetheless, a *psychical researcher* needs better grounds than this to dismiss an ostensibly first-person account; preconceived ideas aside, it deserves to be looked at for traces of fact amid the fiction. The odds seem heavily against the possibility of there being any factual content behind Phantom Hitch-Hiker stories, but this does not furnish an excuse to reject them out of hand. The odds are always against *any* ghost story being factual, purely because all apparitions are impossibilities.

A modern ghost story?

Leaving such contentious matters to one side, we can ponder on the History of the Vanishing Hitchhiker, which was the title chosen by Beardsley and Hankey for their second review of this ubiquitous story. Previously they had decided that although it was not out of the question that the motif(s) had arisen in the pre-motor car age, the geographical distribution and the fact that cars featured in no less than 76 of their 79 examples showed that the modern automobile was a seminal element and that the vehicle was therefore used in the 'primary' story – could this story be but identified.[18] Their next assignment was to examine ghost stories of the past in the hope of locating this catalytic original. Their conclusion was 'if this tale has a historical antecedent we have not yet found it'.[19] Their search revealed only general elements common to European, Greek/Roman tales and American Hitch-Hiker stories – likenesses they felt were *too* general to suggest an intimate relationship. Besides, in these older tales the ghost is always recognized immediately for what it is. As we have seen, one important aspect of Phantom Hitch-Hikers consists of their *not* being readily identifiable as supernatural entities, but as living, unexceptional human persons in need of a lift. Consequently, Beardsley and Hankey were convinced that 'there is a modernity about the elements and the essence of the story . . . which sets it off sharply from the tales of the past. The most significant of the modern elements is the hitch-hiker's successful masquerading as a human being.'[20]

This element, they thought, is rare in European ghostlore and the few exceptions do not rely upon it for their impact. The ghost who is sufficiently real to pass for human – the kind most commonly reported in early psychical research journals – was not popularized until the end of the nineteenth century.

According to Beardsley and Hankey, the earliest Hitch-Hiker stories (Version A) reached a zenith in tale-telling circles of the late 1920s, while the more flamboyant Version C, whose vampiristic anti-heroines may owe a little to European demon-lovers, seems a product of the following decade. 'Research into extant literature suggests possible sources for specific elements but not for the integral core or spirit of the story.'[21]

The writers also offered internal evidence for the modernity of the Vanishing Hitchhiker. The general acceptance of the motor car and its use for long journeys, the casual intimacy of strangers (the hitch-hiking phenomenon or the pick-up at a dance in C Versions) could only be intelligible to members of a mobile, permissive twentieth-century American) culture. The tale itself is told with the factual brevity of a modern news item (printed or broadcast), where it is *de rigeur* to specify the locality. Though this contrasts with the withholding of witnesses' names – and traditionally these individuals are *never* fully identified – Beardsley and Hankey note that the motorists are classed in terms of their occupations: taxi-drivers, businessmen, doctors, and so on. This is another feature of the modern urban tale, but not of the old rural equivalent, where names are attached to stories even if the passing of years has rendered such identification meaningless to the audience(s) concerned. Again, the comparatively rapid spread of the story across the USA might testify to reliance upon speedy, transcontinental communications media only present in a thoroughly techno-logical culture. This last factor, however, does not prevent localizations (Version B in the Midwest, Version D in Hawaii) and variation of specific details.

Believing that the Hitch-Hiker was both urban and a creation of the 1920s/1930s, Beardsley and Hankey pronounced its last rites: 'the story is dying out. Though still told occasionally, it is no longer a vital and living tale.'[22] That is, it shares the ephemerality of the dirty joke and, unlike the stories derived from primitive communities, new features cannot be built into it without destroying the original fabric. Even so, Beardsley and Hankey did not rule out the possibilty that the Phantom Hitch-Hiker might someday enjoy a revival. Regardless of their literal truth or not, newspaper articles of the 1970s would imply that their estimate was not mistaken.

Beardsley and Hankey's research into the origins of the Hitch-Hiker does not appear to have encompassed Alfred Sutro's 'own invention' – the weeping child-ghost which, he affirmed, imposed on not a few over-credulous listeners.[23] Sutro's ersatz apparition is not a typical Phantom Hitch-Hiker, yet it conforms strictly to the 'tale told as true' formula and certain elements in it correspond closely with stories already observed as part of this road-ghost's tradition; in particular her wringing wet clothes and tearful inarticulateness are reminiscent of the unhappy Southampton female, not to mention the drowned specimens popular in Hawaii.[24]

Although he does not attach a date to his fabrication, Sutro's little yarn bears a thematic resemblance to the Version C stories which Beardsley and Hankey believe arose in the 1930s. This means that, sincere as his claim to originality may have been, the playwright cannot also be credited with creation of that first and seminal Phantom Hitch-Hiker tale for which the California duo sought in vain. This they believed to have been along the lines of the address-giving spirit found in the Version A stories dating from the 1920s, whereas Sutro's tale substitutes for this characteristic others found in the C variant of the following decade. And thanks to other folklorists' pursuit of the ghost's ancestors, it now appears that the Phantom Hitch-Hiker is not only older than Alfred Sutro and his own invention, but *far* older than Beardsley and Hankey conceived it might be.

While respecting the findings that led Beardsley and Hankey to the conclusion that the Phantom Hitch-Hiker is a fundamentally modern story (bewailing also their inability to track down an undoubtedly relevant pre-twentieth-century original), it is permissible to challenge that basic premise. The accoutrements of Hitch-Hiker incidents may sound unique to our day and age – the focus on the automobile especially – but the *situation* itself is timeless.

Evidence for this can be found in Andrew MacKenzie's entertaining guide to the peoples and customs of Romania, *Dracula Country*. Writing on the theme of 'corporeal ghosts' – ghosts who, behaving in life-like manner, succeed in passing themselves off as human – Mr MacKenzie cites an English ballad featuring a girl who is given a lift to her door on *horseback* by her recently-deceased lover.[25] This obscure opus is 'The Suffolk Wonder' and it carries the explicit subtitle, 'Or, a Relation of a Young Man, who, a month after his death, appeared to his Sweetheart, and carried her on horseback behind him for forty miles in two hours, and was never seen after but in his grave'. The editor/compiler, John Glyde junior, says the work was taken from a 1723-25 tri-volume anthology of old ballads and that it bears 'a considerable resemblance to the celebrated German ballad of Leonore, by Burger'.[26]

For good measure, the spectral lover is also a token-leaver. *En route* he borrows the girl's handkerchief to bind round his aching head. Sure enough, when the alarmed parents exhume the corpse:

> Affrighted, then they did behold
> His body turning unto mould;
> And though he had a month been dead
> This handkerchief was 'bout his head.

'The Suffolk Wonder' contains the essential elements of a Hitch-Hiker story. The ghost is unrecognizable as such and takes from the main witness an item of apparel that ultimately corroborates the reality of the experience, as well as the fact that the rider and the corpse were/are the same. This, as Beardsley and Hankey established, is a characteristic of the Version C story, as is the vampiristic destruction of the innocent, human travelling-companion:

> This thing unto her then they told
> And the whole truth they did unfold;
> She was thereat so terrify'd,
> And grieved, that she quickly dy'd.

Most significant, the living and the dead share the same means of locomotion, which happens to be the most practical and custom-sanctioned mode of transport for the times.

Finally, Swedish researcher Sven Rosen recently referred me to an account that irrefutably demonstrates that the Phantom Hitch-Hiker is neither an intrinsically modern nor American story. He located this version in a manuscript held by a Linköping library; its title (*Om the tekn och widunder som föregingo thet liturgiske owäsendet*) translates as *On the signs and wonders preceding the liturgic broil*. The author, Joan Petri Klint (d. 1608) is described by Mr Rosen as 'the Swedish portent-collector'. Readers will soon appreciate why the following tale would have awakened the interest of a writer who specialized in such matters.

In February 1602 an unnamed vicar and two farmers were travelling back from the Candlemas fair in Västergötland. (Mr Rosen notes that at this time of the year the vehicle they used must have been a sleigh.) On the road to Vadstena they were accosted by a 'nice' and 'lovely' female dressed like a serving-girl, who asked for (and was given) a ride. At a wayside halting-station they all alighted to get some food; the girl, however, only wanted something to drink. A jug of beer was procured for her. The vicar observed she did not take it up and found it was filled with malt. A second jug mysteriously changed from beer to acorns and a third – apparently under the vicar's nose – to blood. At this point the serving-girl pronounced (as if interpreting these omens): 'There will be good crops this year. There will be enough fruits of the trees. There will also be many wars and plague'. With which she vanished.

We can immediately identify this as a very early but wholly characteristic Hitch-Hiker narrative. The supernatural entity assumes the form of a credible human being (a serving girl). She hitches a lift in the standard form of conveyance for the time and geographical area (a sleigh); she does not disappear from this vehicle but from the close proximity of the witnesses (cf. the girl in the C variant stories). Above all, she voices a prophecy of immediate interest to her captive audience: a Version B Hitch-Hiker effect. The feats of transmuting 'good beer' into the symbolic malt, acorns and blood, no less than her vanishing, support the parahuman reliability of her prophecy. Also in the established B-Version mould (though Mr Rosen says he cannot be certain), there is no evidence that her oracular statements came true.

What matters most is the sheer antiquity of this story. In her paper, 'Jesus on the Thruway' (see Chapter Seven) Professor Fish cites *Acts* 8: 26-40 as an early Hitch-Hiker account; the apostle Philip boards the chariot of the Ethiopian eunuch, converts him to Christianity and is then 'caught away' by the Spirit – in effect, he vanishes or is "teleported" to Azotus. Yet the analogy between this biblical extract and Beardsley and Hankey's collection seems less intrinsic than the one offered by Klint, who must have written it between 1602-1608. It may not only be the earliest 'perfect' Hitch-Hiker tale; its dating may even suggest that the Californian folklorists were not correct in thinking the seminal Hitch-Hiker narrative to have been a Version A (address-giving ghost) model. It is just possible that the road-ghost evolved from, or at any rate came into being after some form of travelling/vanishing prophet story close to Klint's lovely, beer-drinking serving-girl.

It also throws into a new light a UPI report widely taken up by the world's press almost 300 years after the vicar's alleged encounter on the road to Vadstena. Papers as widely scattered as the UK's *Guardian* and the *Schenectady Gazette* (New York) of 31 October 1980 or the *Japan Times* for 1 November related that police in or near Ekenassjon, southern Sweden, were alarmed by repeated cases of dangerous driving as citizens ignored traffic signals to avoid a young male Hitch-Hiker who spoke of the Second Coming. The report's final sentence – a reference to the identical-sounding Arkansas 'prophetic' of a few month's before – reads almost like a confession: as if the writer accepted that someone would detect that the Swedish case had been lifted from the American media and relocated in the customary folklore manner. Alternatively, the open mention of the Little Rock story may have been an invitation for perceptive readers to see through the hoax.

Certainly, the appearance of this tale with its nameless police spokesmen and denials of drunkeness on behalf of equally anonymous witnesses – all utterly conventional attributes of the motif – was suspiciously well coordinated with Hallowe'en. A hoax perpetrated across the international wire services to fit the 'seasonal mood' is not unlikely. Yet it remains interesting that the hoaxers (if any) should have selected a Hitch-Hiker story for their attempt. One wonders whether he, she, or they had any awareness of the Swedish prototype set down by Joan Petri Klint nearly three centuries before.

The Phantom Hitch-Hiker as we know it today is simply the latest updating on an antique theme, not a modernistic one. Professor Louis C. Jones, who believed the Vanishing Hitch-hiker to be neither essentially modern nor of specifically urban/metropolitan parentage, declared:

There have been for some time in Europe and America stories of supernatural hitchhikers who have joined drivers of horse-drawn vehicles for brief journeys and then disappeared. The nonghostly motifs have tended to die out and the more vigorous ghostlore has adapted itself to the changes of transportational environment, as the horse gave way to the auto and bus.[27]

Bilocation and relocation
Efforts to create for the Phantom Hitch-Hiker a lengthy historical pedigree may seem to push the ghost still further away from the factual world of parapsychology. Even were the lineage of this particular road-ghost of no more than academic interest, that attempt would still enter into any rounded discussion which purports to look at the evidence for *and* against the newspapers' assertions that it 'really happens'. As a result of the preceding pages, it seems fair to say that the Phantom Hitch-Hiker is an exceedingly well-known, oft-told story; now to this can be added that it is even older – or better-preserved – than some folklorists have believed. Neither factor is irrelevant to the contention that people have literally experienced outrageously-fictional encounters with passengers who disappear without warning or logic. Taken together, they may even turn out to reconcile the contradiction between a person undergoing in real life an adventure which is known to rank among the inventions of folklore. But more of that later.

*   *   *   *

On 19 June 1907 Andrew Lang read to members of the Folk-Lore Society a suggestively-titled essay on '"Death's Deeds": A Bilocated Tale' – a discussion of two widely-segregated accounts of unusual (perhaps paranormal) movements of coffins inside sealed vaults.[28] Both are well known to psychical researchers, who usually interpret them in terms of poltergeists, undiscovered natural causes or ingenious human agency. Lang found it odd that there should be two such very similar reports of this kind. Despite his awareness of the curious duplication of poltergeist phenomena the world over, he felt bound to ask whether the account of the 1844 disturbances in the Buxhoewden Vault at Ahrensburg on the island of Oesel owed not a little to the earlier, more famous and better-documented 'moving coffins' of Chase Vault, Christchurch in Barbados. 'Did the self-same strange thing happen twice, or more frequently on either side of the Atlantic, within some twenty years, or is the European narrative a deliberate plagiarism from West Indian facts?'[29]

Behind his speculation was the knowledge that a tale, true or invented, can be pigeon-holed, saved up and relocated by a story-teller with its original ambiance exchanged for a new one, which gives a fresh lease of life to what was often a moribund episode. When the stages in the process of transference are indistinguishable, the student of folklore is left with a bilocated story, and (as in the case of Lang and the over-active coffins) it is difficult to decide who undertook the relocation or when.

Transference of a story from one locality (or country) to another can also enliven a flagging tale of roughly similar theme. A case in point is the Mexican legend of 'La Llorona' – the Weeping Woman – whom tradition recalls drowned her child (or children) in a river and whose spirit could be heard and sometimes seen henceforth on the banks, bemoaning her lost one(s) in piteous, eerie manner. When immigrants crossed the Rio and settled in the USA they took La Llorona along with them; she, too, found a new home far from her native climes, even so far north as Indiana, where folklorist Philip Brandt George detected her in 1972. And although the small Calumet River close to Cudehey (a former suburb of Gary with a mainly Mexican population) must have been very different from the original scene of her rash action, she began to haunt the spot in the same old style.

Oddly enough, though, La Llorona found herself in competition with an already established ghost – a Phantom Hitch-Hiker of the type recorded so well by Beardsley and Hankey, a woman in white who had lost her family (in a fire or car accident) or her own life (killed in an automobile crash or murdered on her wedding night by her husband). Far from counteracting each other, these potential rivals compromised or coalesced in a way that makes George's paper fascinating reading.[30]

Alerted by the presence of thirteen variants on the Cline Avenue Ghost in the Folklore Archives of Indiana University, George visited the Calumet region to seek material in the form of on-the-spot interviews with oral informants. He found that Cudehey had ceased to exist as a residential zone, but amid the storage tanks and bleak, smog-wrapped industrial complexes reaching towards the river the White Lady still appeared and vanished, notably on the stretch of Cline Avenue around the junction marking the former site of the now-demolished suburb. Or rather, she had done until quite recently, according to what the informants had to say.

The Ghost of Cline Avenue is an important illustration of a relocated story and of a Phantom Hitch-Hiker in transition. It is an amalgam: a combination of two ghostly motifs, neither of which fully sublimates the other. As regards the Phantom Hitch-Hiker format, the tales are of the 'truncated' or incomplete variety; the crucial element of identification (of the ghost) is missing, and that in itself is worthy of comment. The encounter – always between a male motorist and a woman in white at roughly the same point on Cline Avenue and always at night – and the vanishing of the back seat passenger within a short space of time are standard for the motif; but there is never a suggestion of the 'witness' being given an address to follow up, which makes it impossible to say who the lady may be (or more correctly, who she may have been). In the best oral tradition, these stories are made to seem credible by the statement that a team of television, radio and newspaper men once visited the scene in the hope of seeing and recording the ghost, thereby encouraging large numbers of people to join the unrewarded hunt. George found several informants, including one police officer, who testified that this search actually took place as described, though the estimated date of the event was subject to fluctuations.

It was the folklorist's conjecture that the original Cline Avenue Ghost had been a Phantom Hitch-Hiker who asked to be taken to an address in Cudehey. The demolition projects which transformed the character of that area soon made it illogical for any Hitch-Hiker to want to go there; they had in effect made the White Lady homeless, in the sense that storytellers no longer regarded Cudehey as a place where people *lived*. The identification-by-address motif becoming obsolete, this formerly important segment of the tale was dropped, with the result that the story dangled in the air, an incomplete entity. This allowed alternative endings to appear – multivariate endings featuring accidents, murders and other categories of tragedy which suggested the ghost's earthly identity. The most polished of these was taken from the already-developed motif of La Llorona, the woman who drowned her child(ren). When the Mexican inhabitants moved to surrounding districts, they fed this latest avatar of the Cline Avenue Ghost back into the folklore of Calumet.

Mr George does not investigate the possibility that any of these incidents might have been based on anything approaching fact, and it may be significant that most of his informants maintained a certain indifference to or disbelief in the story, though it was part of the convention to cite the media interest as evidence that some aspects of it were accepted as 'true'. Taken as a group, these Cline Avenue tales can be seen as a conglomerate example of how relocation and reworking of material can graft new characteristics onto a venerable tradition.

This does not rule out the idea that the presence of common factors – here, belief in supernatural beings who assume human form and the general use of a custom-sanctioned mode of transport (horse, wagon, motor-car) – can give rise to the same story in different geographical locations, the inhabitants of which never come into contact with each other. Nor, according to Lang, would the existence of similar ghost narratives across the world necessarily act as proof of their fictional nature. When dealing with poltergeists, for instance, he would say that the numbers of comparable accounts did not signify dissemination, bilocation or independent creation, but quite simply that widely-spaced observers had recorded a phenomenon that behaved the same way everywhere – a strong argument in favour of its validity. Applied to the subject of this book, it would be *theoretically* possible to postulate that the Phantom Hitch-Hiker may be seen as a broadly disseminated story, a tale concocted by more than one narrator on more than one occasion, or else as a class of psychic activity that displays itself in more or less the same format all over the world.

Multiple, variant texts, writes Professor Jan Harold Brunvand in his penetrating study of 'urban legends' (which uses the Vanishing Hitchhiker as a kind of keynote typifying the genre) are good evidence against the credibility of the individual story in question: the more variations there are on a 'true tale', the less likely it is to be true.[31] And there is no point in resisting the fact that most Phantom Hitchhikers are disseminations, relocated after the fashion just outlined and passed off as things original, unique, genuine.

It is quite natural that there should be so many similar ghost tales of *all* types, because people are reluctant to let good stories pass into oblivion. Since no one takes these ghosts at more than surface level they are legitimate material wherever and whenever we reciprocate on the topic of the supernatural; moreover, there is a tacit agreement that the basic plot of a story matters more than the incidentals – names, dates, places – which permits these elements to become subject to alteration. Additionally, the streamlined and practically all-embracing power of modern media lends itself to dissemination and relocation of stories in a way not equalled by the mainly oral tradition of previous centuries.

There is nothing that heightens the immediacy of a tale as much as the hint (or assertion) that it took place somewhere known to the circle of listeners. Beardsley and Hankey note that a major convention of the Hitch-Hiker motif is that it stipulates specific places, 'one device used to emphasize the authenticity which adds greatly to the effectiveness of the tale'.[32] Even more prestigious – both to the tale and to the tale-teller – is the statement that 'it happened to me', or failing that, to someone the narrator knows personally and can vouch for. In 13 of Beardsley and Hankey's 79 accounts the encounter was alleged to have befallen a friend and in two others a relative.

It is hard to assess how seriously people will take the assertion that a story is true because it involved a friend of the narrator – or, more likely, a friend of a friend of the narrator (a 'foaf', as Rodney Dale wittily contracts it in his analysis of apocryphal 'true' yet highly unlikely tales[33]). But story-telling has its conventions just as written fiction has, and for reasons of politeness, or for psychological ones, we may be inclined to suspend criticism when we meet these casual attempts at validification. The story is all that really matters, and for his part the narrator must try to reinforce the impression that the events he or she describes actually took place. The end of the story may also carry some conventional corroborative remarks, rather like a seal or guarantee, when the speaker 'proves' the truth of the tale by citing its after-effect on the motorist (goes insane, dies, etc.), or by pointing out that it was printed as a fact by the newspapers. As for ourselves, the listeners, we may discard or accept as we please. Narrator and audience alike may subscribe to Mark Twain's dictum, uttered under similar conditions: 'Stated to me for a fact. I only tell it as I got it. I am willing to believe it. I can believe anything.'[34]

A step beyond folklore?

On consideration of behavioural motifs alone – what the ghost does, the form/appearance it takes – almost every apparition can be reduced to folklore. For example, 'crisis' or 'hour of death' cases, where the apparition seems to represent a visual communication from someone on the verge of quitting an earthly existence at a time and place far removed from the witness, are supported by documentation of such calibre that they not only form the backbone of the claim that people genuinely see phantoms, but for the validity of the paranormal as a whole.[35] The wealth of cross-examination and after-the-event corroboration makes it certain that these veridical apparitions are more than variant, relocated folk-tales; as Lang would have approved, they are more fairly approached as haphazard but recurring events consistently recorded throughout time and space. In short, they are authenticated actualities.

Long before psychical researchers managed to establish them as such, however, these crisis apparitions were already ancient. This makes the motif fair game for the folklorist, too, and recognizing the type in a tale from history or fable – as Lang tracked a purposeful hour of death phantom back across 700 years to a tale in William of Malmesbury[36] – he or she might insist that for all their apparent veracity these incidents are merely reworkings of hoary material. The proofs that the ghosts coincided with or matched verified distant tragedies of which the witnesses were supposedly ignorant does not compensate for the fact that there is no *objective* proof that these percipients truly *did* see the ghosts in the first place; frequently a reader is asked to accept this on the grounds that researchers have established that the tragedy held responsible for the ghost's appearance has been confirmed to have occurred, which is a somewhat circular process of reasoning. To a determined sceptic, the corroborative data produced by investigators relative to this last point is a narrative flourish, something tacked onto the end of a story to give a savour of authenticity in the same way that orally-told stories cite newspaper coverage of supernatural episodes to demonstrate that they 'really happened'.

Thanks to the huge volume of background research undertaken, there seems no danger that crisis apparitions will lose their place in the factual annals of parapsychology. The Phantom Hitch-Hiker is unlikely to acquire that position,

Professor Jan Harold Brunvand of the University of Utah – seen here minus his usual spectacles – places the Vanishing Hitchhiker among the classic urban legends featuring automobiles. (*photograph courtesy of Professor Brunvand*)

though, because the inferences of folklore have discouraged anyone from trying to corroborate so blatantly fictional a tale. 'The status of such urban legends as folklore is unquestionable,' says Professor Brunvand, 'despite the common belief among tellers and listeners that they are truthful accounts, or at least based on actual events . . . It is also surprising that few individuals, other than occasional folklorists or journalists, become curious enough about the alleged firsthand sources to follow the leads back a few steps to the – inevitable – dead end.'[37]

But what if it transpires that the dead end is not so inevitable after all? Suppose for a moment that field research *is* conducted – that it indicates that the supposedly specious testifiers to fact, the elusive witnesses, *could* be traced, or that the police have verified otherwise dubious press allegations that official reports of the phenomenon have been received? Obviously, we can never be in a position to rule out these possibilities *unless* the kind of investigation Professor Brunvand alludes to *is* made. And if it is, we may come to suspect that the habit of lying is more deeply ingrained than the most pessimistic of commentators has suggested – and that the choice of lie (the Hitch-Hiker) has an international appeal. Alternatively, we may suspect that a handful of genuine incidents have been fudged due to competition from a formidably large canon of fictional tales on the same theme.

Comparison of the characteristics discerned by Beardsley and Hankey *et al* with the reported data of recent (1970s) accounts reveals some important divergences between the Phantom Hitch-Hikers of folk-narratives and the allegedly factual item. The Hitch-Hiker of folklore always combines behaviour with purpose, returning to the world of the living in order to haunt the place of her tragic death *and* infallibly giving the witness enough information to check her identity (whereby the relevance of her being on that stretch of road is made clear). As observed in the preceding chapter, some of the 1970s incidents lack this logical patterning; the Nunney and Stanbridge ghosts appeared and vanished without hinting at any motive or purpose, and their relationship with any accidental death rests solely upon conjecture. These open-ended stories cannot lead to the 'parental explanation' because the driver has no information to guide him to any helpful parent. They are inherently closer to the sort of case common in psychical research, where the ghost is often a once-seen and unintelligible event. If we insist that these stories are nonetheless folklore – fragmentary and missing typical details due to unforeseen factors – their atypicality and the 'unforeseen factors' themselves require definition, since the themes of revelation of the passenger's identity and non-living status are integral to the folklore Hitch-Hiker – the whole point of it, some might argue.

It would be foolish to think that incompleteness can be taken on its own as evidence that a story is factual; as the case of the truncated Cline Avenue Ghost shows, lack of the address/ identification submotif(s) may result from local circumstances.

Even so, if other indicators are present this rationalization may not apply.

Another major difference: 'The vanishing hitchhiker is without exception female,' state Beardsley and Hankey.[38] She certainly is in their sample: 47 girls, 14 old women (often of the prophetic kind) and 14 others designated as perhaps one or the other. Masculine counterparts are found only in folklore's Version B tales (post-Beardsley and Hankey); for no immediately obvious reason, however, they appear far more regularly where the story is offered in terms of news-fact. Then there is the matter of dress and accessories; note the usual impracticality of the folklore girl, whose evening dress or flimsy clothes are no match for the nocturnal conditions. This defencelessness, as the authors suggest, may provide the motorist of the story with a reason for stopping to offer the girl a lift – a literary mechanism – and if her individual choice of clothing is thought incongruous, the writers would say that the details 'represent the narrator's fancy at play with his material'.[39] By contrast, the dress of more modern examples does not always reflect this disregard for the elements; some Hitch-Hikers even wear mackintoshes.

Other aspects of the Beardsley and Hankey sample vary less radically yet significantly from what some may tentatively choose to believe are real-life Hitch-Hiker incidents. Contrasting with the essential anonymity of witnesses remarked upon earlier, recent newspaper reports give (as for most kinds of news item) names, ages, occupations and partial addresses of persons involved, sometimes enabling the more energetic researcher to track down the participants.

Lastly, there is the matter of after-the-fact corroboration. Sceptics may dismiss police investigations of Phantom Hitch-Hiker incidents as literary flourishes, further narrative devices to convey an extra flavour of authenticity; the fact that the police (authority figures lending additional credence to the stories, Professor Brunvand points out) 'find nothing' only adds to the supernatural impact. To the contrary, it is irrefutable that the police *have* taken up particular reports, mounting searches or else logging accounts made in the semblance of good faith even when it seemed highly unlikely they would be able to provide a solution for the alleged encounter. There are police statements arising from reports handed in at places as far apart as Nunney, Blue Bell Hill and Stanbridge (Great Britain), Uniondale (South Africa) and Montpellier (France); if this testifies to hoaxers with a strange sense of humour we must add again that they share an internationalized appreciation for comedy and that, by taking the thing seriously, the police forces of the world are participating in the joke.[40] And inconclusive as the searches were preordained to be, the very fact that they were undertaken at all indicates that police involvement is not always a mere turn of the pen or the narrator's final gesture toward oral convention.

Insignificant these differences may appear, yet they spotlight several intriguing developments in the long history of the Phantom Hitch-Hiker. Either a new form of folk-version has evolved, open-ended and inconclusive, with the ghost now paying attention to its 'street credibility' by wearing apposite clothing, contemporary with which some bold persons have been trying to waste the police's time by passing off fabricated folk-yarns as their own, factual experiences. Or there again, perhaps a few of these alleged incidents were founded on a modicum of fact.

The role of the press

For most of us, awareness of Phantom Hitch-Hikers and the like comes with a tantalizingly-brief report in a newspaper. Naturally, we are at liberty to believe it or not, but for anyone who wants to take the thing further there instantly arises the question: how much of what we read in the papers *can* be believed?

Journalists are fair game for the cynics. They are accused of fact-bending, partiality, unscrupulousness and low cunning – nor does that exhaust the list of perjoratives. This reputation of the species without exception is ill-deserved. Journalists (unlike some of their more emotional critics) deal mostly in facts – as they perceive them to be. Of course, between the fact and the writer's perception of it can come a great and troublesome gulf that leads to misconstructions and misinterpretations. It is also true that not only do news reporters tend to give supernaturally-flavoured stories a rather flippant treatment – the Ghost Story as Entertainment style of presentation – but indubitable 'urban legends' do occasionally appear as honest-to-goodness truisms. Newsmen with a pronounced sense of humour may initiate a few of these (some of which are circulated internationally by wire services), passing off old 'whale tumour stories' as verified events, and repeating what they know or else suspect to be a WTS notified to them by informants. Such commemoration in print actually reinforces the belief that the story in question is genuine, as we have already seen.

That said, while a newspaper account of a haunting may not mean that the facts of the case are precisely as written, it can alert researchers to the *allegation* that something unusual is in the offing – something perhaps falling within those researchers' field. The only realistic way of deciding the matter is to use the press account as a guide and *then* attempt to address the balance of truth and fiction, if need be. Fact has a funny way of imitating fiction; parts of dead mice *do* wind up in coke bottles, as per the urban legend. Does this mean that the story might be based upon antique fact or that hoaxers are arranging for it to come to life?[41]

Nor – contrary to what some outside journalism may think – are pressmen enamoured of old news, which as far as the more responsible reporters are concerned is a contradiction in terms. If the Phantom Hitch-Hiker is simply a relocated tale *and nothing else*, how has the press remained ignorant of its bogus quality? Is this naive ignorance, or (far worse) knowing ignorance?

Many psychical researchers maintain a studied caution toward anything the papers have to say on their subject, largely from the belief that journalists are incapable of describing such things without melodrama or exaggeration. Although it is sometimes urged that ghosts enter the bracket of 'human interest' stories, this does not mean that matters of corroboration are automatically thrust aside. "'We take these stories with a pinch of salt,'" as one newsman told me when we were both working (though from different motives) on a fairly typical case of ghost-seeing.

Sensationalism in the presentation of hauntings, poltergeists and the like is usually a result of simplification rather than of outright invention of details or artificial colouring of such as are already present. One common approach or 'angle' which can have that effect is selective quoting – in a ghost story, this might mean a direct statement from the testimony of a witness with little or no independent corroboration to balance the picture. Again one has to be cautious in accusing the journalist of distortion when he/she resorts to this technique; it may be an inescapable outcome of the situation. All investigators know the problems surrounding evaluation of a case where the only witness or witnesses were the persons actually (perhaps emotionally as well as physically) involved. Short of 'seeing something' himself, the interviewer has few positive and no infallible means of verifying the account since there are no objective means of proving that *any* incident recalled by a witness took place as described.

Can we then blame a journalist who, with little time at his disposal, will handle a Phantom Hitch-Hiker sighting wholly reliant on the word of a single witness in the easiest manner possible – by quoting without comment that person's own version of the events? Whatever its faults, this is a direct and captivating way of writing up the story, with the powerful bonus that all 'It happened to me' experiences possess. Newspaper accounts of the Hitch-Hiker are nearly always the facts *as the motorist proclaims them to have been*. Subsidiary or substantiating evidence comes only from the police spokeman's assurance that they are treating the matter seriously, that the man was not drunk, and (perhaps) that other reports like it have been received in the past.

So, noting their limitations, and not ruling out the possibility that on occasions newspapers may rehash old stories, having first given them local habitations and different names, these published accounts might be used as an indication that something is going on. It is unlikely, but not altogether impossible, that in *some* of the cases described the witnesses experienced, or (equally valid) *thought* they experienced, the uncanny events attributed to their names by the press.

But how accurate a reflection of the events are these reports? At what stages if at all do the artificial colourings and paring down of inconveniently ambiguous details come on the scene?

Perhaps we shall be able to decide after a trip to Somerset for an on-site review of a Phantom Hitch-Hiker who made the national papers only a few years ago.

THREE:
NUNNEY EXCURSIONS

Situated about three miles southwest of Frome, the small but picturesque Somersetshire village of Nunney offers many attractions to summer visitors. Several, like the impressively-battered castle, have a definite publicity value,[1] but in August 1977, when inhabitants were preparing to celebrate the Silver Jubilee of Queen Elizabeth II, publicity of a different sort descended on this normally quiet village. As reported in the national press, Nunney was gripped in a panic that had turned its ordinary citizens into ghost-seers and ghost-hunters. To be more precise, a 'middle-aged' phantom was alleged to be hitching lifts on the road leading to Frome and disappearing. Here, as reconstructed from the printed sources, is the full story.

A likely tale
At an unspecified time and date, a twenty-year-old decorator, whom I shall call Mr Evans, seemed destined to become a laughing-stock in the town of Frome when news of his ghostly encounters in 'a lonely country lane' were recounted by several newspapers.[2] He had picked up a man on the Frome-Nunney Road because the fellow looked as if he wanted a lift; the traveller climbed into the back seat and Mr Evans locked the door after him. The only conversation during the drive featured the hitch-hiker's repeated comment on how cold it was (a remark which perhaps hints at the conclusion of the story) and a question from Mr Evans that elicited no response because – as he immediately discovered – the man had vanished. *The Weekly News* of 20 August 1977 gives the supplementary information that the driver had not heard the car door being opened or closed *en route*.

Frome Police Station is conveniently located for anyone wishing to report an unusual incident on the road up from Nunney; the motorist merely takes the first turning left after reaching the crest of Gibbet Hill, which marks the point of entry into the outskirts of the town proper. Mr Evans duly made his way to the station, told his story and (according to one journalist) was given a breathalyzer test, though he had not been drinking. This sequence of events was later confirmed to have taken place by a police spokesman, who delineated the witness as 'a highly distraught motorist'. Searches of the lane proved negative. The incident might have been dismissed or relegated to folklore without further ado had not Mr Evans claimed to have undergone a *second* encounter with the *same* apparition in the *same* spot, some time afterwards – precisely how long afterwards we are not told. The man was standing in the centre of the road and in the effort to avoid him the decorator skidded into a lamp-post. When he got out of his car the cause of the accident 'was not there'.

Already we can appreciate the characteristics of the Nunney Hitch-Hiker – and also the absence of certain details that might add to our understanding of the alleged incidents. For instance, the *Sunday Express* report of 14 August 1977 does not offer a description of the man/ghost, nor indicate where he was picked up; the reference to the lamp-post perhaps encourages the supposition that the second Evans encounter took place close to the outskirts of *either* Nunney *or* Frome, yet it is hard to decide between the two because we are also left uninformed as to the direction in which the witness was travelling. But before considering some of the problems arising from comparison of accounts in three nationally-circulated sources, let us return to the story.

The main angle of the *Sunday Express* article was not centred upon the experiences of Mr Evans, but on the rumour, confusion and reaction they had provoked among the inhabitants of Nunney. It was said that other persons were suffering from unwanted passengers who materialized in the back seats of their cars when they travelled along the lane. The only evidence for this phenomenon came from council purchasing officer Mr Owen Hillier, who said he could not help glancing over his shoulder to see if anyone was behind him when he used the road late at night, and from a 46-year-old Frome lady named Valerie McPherson, who was slightly more emphatic in identifying a 'strange feeling that there was someone in the car' on one unaccompanied nocturnal drive. She was too apprehensive to turn around to check whether her fears had any foundation.

By this time elderly pedestrians were alleged to be avoiding the road after dark; drivers were similarly said to be using a longer (but phantom-free) route to Nunney, presumably either the A361 or the road via Lower Whately and Egford, to the north. It is at this stage that the reporter introduces the group of Nunney Vigilantes whose doings were softly burlesqued in Chapter One.

Reports had seemingly filtered back to the organizers of the Silver Jubilee celebrations to the effect that the hitch-hiking ghost would deter some visitors from attending the festivities. Consequently a group of local residents formed patrols and bore noise detectors, tape recorders, light meters plus (in the words of the *Sunday People*) 'a special ghost-grabbing net' along the road at night in an effort to alleviate the situation.

Mr Ron Macey, a building society manager and Secretary of the Silver Jubilee Committee, was quoted in some detail; he was the man who instigated the idea of the patrols and was moreover able to confirm the part about the ghost's detrimental influence on potential visitors. ('"That's when I decided we should form patrols to get to the bottom of it."') He himself was wary of the lane at night and would not stop to offer anyone a lift there. Predictably, the ghost-hunters had only very limited success. The closest they came to the apparition was a meeting with two persons who had seen a shadowy form in the lane some days previously – they thought it *might* have been the ghost.

The *Sunday People* concentrated entirely on the vigilantes (whom it numbered at twenty-four) without so much as a mention of the Evans encounters. It quoted Mr Macey to great effect on the seriousness of the situation and, even better, police Superintendant John Lee, who observed that there had been odd happenings along the road. *The Weekly News* article opened with the first of Mr Evans's experiences but the second, firmly attributed to him in the *Sunday Express*, seems to have become detached and altered; the police were said to have responded to an accident report to find a car lodged in a hedge, where it had ended up after an *unnamed* driver swerved to avoid a man in the road who was trying to flag him down. This sounds too much like Mr Evans' second harrowing experience to be coincidental, but more on this presently. One unique element in this version of the story is that the drivers had described their unearthly passenger in the same manner: as a middle-aged man in a check jacket.

Finally all is lost in conjecture. For example, there is the less than helpful aside that Judge Jeffreys hanged his victims along this road and that the creaking of gibbets can be heard on some nights – though as Steve Moore remarks in his *Fortean Times* summary of the case, it does not seem likely that any of the casualties from the Bloody Assizes would have gone in for check jackets.[3] Nor, for that matter, would they have had much awareness of motor-cars.

One week after its coverage of the Evans double-encounter and aftermath, the *Sunday Express* printed an intriguing envoi in the shape of a letter from former heavy goods driver George Gardiner.[4] Casting his mind back across a gulf of about thirty years, the writer could well remember that one or two of his fellow drivers had reported seeing what may have been the same ghost in about the same place. Thirty years . . .

By the end of the month the dangers of the Frome-Nunney Road were not so much ghostly as goonish.[5] Twice in two weeks police received complaints from motorists who had met – not the Phantom Hitch-Hiker, but his man-made impersonator. Driving into the village at a narrow point flanked by high walls, Mr David Harrison of Egford was taken by surprise when something white flapped out from the tree-tops – something which was on strings. Superintendent Lee was again the man to whom the press turned for informed comment. The character of this latest piece of 'phenomena' was not at issue, since the 'ghost' seen by Mr Harrison had turned out to be a white sheet with a black-taped grin affixed to the region intended for its face; but Superintendent Lee left the apparition's constructors in no doubt as to his opinion of their handiwork. The police could see the funny side of the thing, he said, but the joke had gone far enough. Motorists being startled into swerving by home-made phantoms was no laughing matter and he wanted those responsible to take note of his warning. Presumably they did, for there are no further reports of pseudo-spectres – and indeed, none of the allegedly-genuine article, either.

This may be a good point to retreat from the published accounts concerning the haunted road and to deliberate as to whether or not the grin on the face of the artificial ghost was justified.

In the footsteps of the Phantom Hitch-Hiker

Frome police are more accustomed to receiving eye-witness reports of UFOs than to hearing about Phantom Hitch-Hikers – a legacy, no doubt, of Mr Arthur Shuttlewood's numerous books on extraterrestrial hyperactivity over nearby Warminster. Nonetheless, as I learned during a visit to the scene of the purported haunt some three years after the newspaper coverage just presented, the press did not manufacture the detail of motorists coming off the Frome-Nunney Road to report vanishing passengers: it *had* happened and more than once.

'We've had people come in here in a state of virtual hysteria,' the duty officer told me, with no trace of sarcasm; he was quick to add that although the police often use the 'haunted road' none of *their* drivers has ever come upon the mysterious Hitch-Hiker. Thus it seems that the reports alluded to in the newspapers were genuine – not journalistic attempts to infuse credibility into an unbelievable story. What those distraught-motorist reports might mean is a very different problem. The officer felt that the haunting may be somehow related to the affirmed existence of a gibbet in the area, commemorated both in the name of a hill and a local farm. He was less keen on the Judge Jeffreys connection; that notorious gentlemen did not confine himself to this corner of Somerset, after all.

Below Gibbet Hill the Frome-Nunney road drops away and

The author poses somewhat unconvincingly as a Hitchhiker on Gibbet Hill, a place-name that recurs constantly throughout the press treatments of the Nunney case. (*photograph by Sheila Donaghy*)

becomes a pleasant country lane, sheltered by stretches of hedgerow. Even so, it is not exactly the placid little byeway evoked in the press reports; traffic, heavy in both directions, sweeps past the narrow verges at high speed and it is a rapidly-reached conclusion that this factor alone is sufficient cause for pedestrians to avoid the road at night, even discounting possible clashes with ghosts. In Nunney itself I heard a succinct and irritatingly vague story which associated the Hitch-Hiker with the spirit of an American serviceman killed in a car crash. The suggestion was thrown out in a manner that indicated the speaker 'only told it as he got it'; all the indications were that local residents are somewhat confused as to the ghost's identity and their impressions – perhaps also those of the press – may have been influenced by a number of early published or oral speculations on this aspect of the story.

One convenient guide to the inchoate history of the tale-cum-legend appears in *Local Ghosts. True Stories, Odd Happenings* by Margaret Royal and Ian Girvan.[6] This takes us a little deeper into the topography of the area, for the incidents – note use of the plural – are said to have happened on the road between Nunney and Critchill, with the phantom traveller requesting to be taken to a place not mentioned in any of the accounts we have studied so far. Since it is likely that one or both of the authors collected their version of the tale from *in situ* sources, this variant is interesting. Critchill is the name given to land on and around Gibbet Hill, where Ordnance Survey Sheet ST74 locates a farm and a house with that title. The short Royal/ Girvan entry relates that three motorists at some belated hour of the night have (separately, of course) picked up a man who wanted to go to Nunney Catch, a small collection of buildings just south of Nunney itself; each time he vanished before they reached this destination. One incident was reported to the Frome police and another resulted in hospital treatment for the motorist concerned.[7]

Needless to say, the writers omit any reference to the *names* of the three victims, but the brief account is not without value. As the booklet appeared in 1976, it gives a clue that the Phantom Hitch-Hiker of Nunney had permeated the local consciousness some time before the press seized upon and described Mr Evans' alarming double-encounter (in the following year). The same text also states that the three motorists were in agreement as to the appearance of the Hitch-Hiker: male, aged between thirty and forty and wearing a check jacket.

At this stage Nunney might appear to have been acting host to yet another relocated Vanishing Hitch-Hiker with the pre-1977 tales of the road-ghost in a check jacket providing substance for later versions. Yet the police involvement seems to refute the theory that this was the usual case of all talk and no action; far from being a conventional narrative device inserted for effect, it is clear that official reports of the phenomenon were actually received. However, to present anything remotely resembling evidence that the story rests on a more factual basis still – and of course, evidence is not *proof* – one has to go back to the source material and attempt to fill in the more inadmissibly blank passages of the account as it has just been told.

Good stories start at the beginning, but one problem about the Nunney story is that it is almost impossible to deduce where that beginning may have been. The height of the ghost's career was August 1977, when it moved up from local or regional celebrity to the eagerly-coveted columns of three national publications; in spite of this there are grounds for thinking (as the Royal/Girvan booklet indicates) that it had been reported active before this date.

The *Sunday People* (14 August 1977) said that the villagers believed the Hitch-Hiker had first been seen two years before (1975). This conflicts with 'guesstimates' in other sources,[8] but it is supported by a short yet important article in the *Bath and West Evening Chronicle* for 14 April 1975, entitled, 'Phantom Hiker'. The story, with its references to Critchill and Nunney Catch, echoes the version in the aforementioned Royal/Girvan booklet, though it does not stipulate that three motorists were separately involved, nor is there any reference to a check jacket. On the other hand, it features one stable element of the Nunney mythos plus a recurrent subsidiary: a frightened motorist is supposed to have reported an incident of this type to the police and the locality is assumed to have been the scene of mass hangings by Judge Jeffreys. These two motifs are consistently mentioned throughout the paper's coverage of the Nunney case.

So we may be disposed to think that the sightings date from at least 1975, or perhaps slightly before. However, the *Sunday Express* letter from George Gardiner, the ex-lorry driver who suggested that one or two other employees of the Avonmouth company for which he had worked had also encountered the ghost in this area, might push the phantasmal record back even further: by as much as thirty years. If, of course, we not only believe the sightings were genuine, but that the same apparition was involved; we are dealing with one person's recollection of events said to have taken place some *three decades* ago, which makes it hard to respond positively. And the story Mr Gardiner offered by way of explaining the haunt – the after-effects of a dying cyclist's curse on all motorists when one had knocked him from his machine – is even more antique than the Man in the Check Jacket could claim to be. It may be found in many road-ghost tales from different parts of Britain and is not inevitably attached to the Hitch-Hiker genre. Here it manages to add another dimension of confusion to a case already troubled by allusions to Judge Jeffreys, deceased American serviceman and a few other incidentals besides.

Staying with Mr Gardiner, a slight variation in his version of the tale occurred when he recited it for the *Bath and West Evening Chronicle*, a paper that paid close attention to many phases of the Nunney ghost-hunt. In the article of 23 August 1977 (hot on the heels of the *Sunday Express* letter) he is quoted as saying that the actual cyclist fatality *occurred* about thirty years ago, but the experiences of his workmates are not dated.[9] The journalist contrasts this interpretation with that of Mr Owen Hillier, the council purchasing officer mentioned in the first *Express* account, who has been a Nunney resident for over fifty years. As Mr Hillier speaks of how he had heard his father talk of the ghost – and how his father's father had done so as well – the Nunney phantom recedes still deeper into the impenetrable depths of time and folk-memory. The writer preferred Mr Gardiner's dying cyclist to Judge Jeffreys on the basis that the story/theory was more consonant with the twentieth-century characteristics of the apparition. Mr Hillier hesitantly mentioned a tale of an innocent man hanged for murder, but added that it might be 'imagination'.

Homicide and miscarriage of justice is not a motif that figures strongly in Phantom Hitch-Hiker stories. Mention of it here illustrates how readily local tales can become entwined; Mr Hillier's remark probably relates to an inevitably diffuse legend concerning a man who came home to find his wife murdered (and who was presumably hung for the crime). This event may have been recorded in the name given to a stretch of Fordbury Water north-northwest of Nunney: Murder Combe. Local historian Mr Michael McGarvie told me that the name is at least 1000 years old, being mentioned in an Anglo-Saxon charter,[10] but he knows of no actual record of any tragedy connected with the place. Despite the feeling of one member of Frome Public Library's staff that it is a creepy spot there appears no obvious connection between Murder Combe and the Nunney Hitch-Hiker.

Yet it seems that the Nunney Ghost *is* rooted in local history. As already noted, newspaper reports of 1976/77 made free with references to Judge Jeffreys and the Frome gibbet; the historical discrepancy of any victim of either (or both) wearing a checked jacket appears to have gone unnoticed. Jeffreys, we also noted in passing, is not especially connected with Frome, although he may have ordered some of its parishioners to be executed there following trial in another part of the country. 'Courts were held in the larger towns, though hangings took place locally,' affirms Mr Kingsley Palmer, a research anthropologist and collector of Wessex's oral folk-tales, who was brought up in Somerset. Having summarized Jeffreys' judiciary travels in the region not long after the battle of Sedgemoor on 6 July 1685, he remarks that historical fact and popular belief do not always tally because 'oral tradition tends to view events in a different light. It describes Jeffreys visiting all sorts of places to which in fact he never went.'[11]

As far as this particular haunting is concerned, the conjectural Judge Jeffreys connection is annoyingly vague but predictably endurable. An article by Mervyn Hancock in the *Somerset Standard*, written at the zenith of the ghost-hunting patrols, provides another snippet on Jeffreys which historians may care to confirm or reject: it is stated that the Judge held an assize in a room at the George Inn, Nunney and that the present licensee discovered a dungeon where condemned rebels were held (prior to hanging in what is now the pub garden) during renovations. Of course the George is haunted and the sound of wind-propelled gallows ropes is described as commonplace.[12] Elsewhere we read of Jeffreys hanging victims along the actual Frome-Nunney Road with the same swinging-gibbet sound effects henceforth to be heard.

At some stage we have to concede that attempts to establish the exact moment of the Phantom Hitch-Hiker's debut are not likely to meet with success; the ever-retreating date is enveloped in mists of folk-memory. Perhaps this piece of data is not crucial; we may accept that a version (or versions) of the story was/were current at various times, with reports of sightings reaching a peak in 1976/77. It seems more profitable to concentrate upon the latter period and most notably on the peculiar double-encounter which brought a driver into contact with the Phantom Hitch-Hiker (twice), the police (ditto) and with a lamp-post (once only). These were the Evans incidents, the only ones for which we have a witness's name and first-person statements. Even here we find a disappointing number of hiatuses and contradictions.

The Evans Encounters reviewed

It would be convenient if the Evans incidents could be divorced from all the others alleged to have featured the Nunney Hitch-Hiker but this is practically impossible. Nor did it prove possible for me to interview the person best-placed to resolve many of the conundrums concerning these incidents – Mr Evans himself; the net result being that what follows is based upon the published material with additional data supplied in confidence from someone who knows the witness extremely well. This is not an ideal situation – how far short of ideal can be seen from the next few paragraphs.

Bearing in mind what I learned at Frome Police Station – 'We've had people in here in a state of virtual hysteria' – it is evident that Mr Evans was not the only person to have formally reported an encounter with a vanishing passenger. It is hard to decide whether he was the *first* to have made such a claim, and even harder to judge whether he was the driver who allegedly ran his car into a hedge in trying to avoid the jaywalking apparition.

The car-in-hedge episode recurs throughout press treatments of the Nunney case from the *Bath and West Evening Chronicle* of 14 April 1975 onwards. In setting the occurrence the previous year, another article in the same paper (4 August 1977) asserted that there had been frequent complaints following this incident – so many that the police had mounted an unfruitful search along the road. Superintendent John Lee was quoted on a perturbed driver who alerted them on the off-chance that the vanishing hitch-hiker had fallen from his car; the witness's name is unfortunately not given. This incident was alluded to in the paper's later (23 August) coverage of the mystery, by which time Superintendent Lee's words, slightly abridged, had been repeated in the *Sunday People*. In between, Mervyn Hancock's *Somerset Standard* piece placed the event the year before (1976) and noted that other motorists had spoken of similar ones to the Frome police.

All this really tells us is that several drivers are believed to have reported meeting the Hitch-Hiker – but we are left to wonder who they were; and that one frequently spoken-of episode involved a motorist who drove into a hedge while attempting to avoid such an encounter. At the start of this chapter a close similarity was surmised between this accident and the sequel to Mr Evans's effort to evade the presumptive ghost, whom (it will be recalled) he had already met some time prior to this accident; the outcome of this evasion was a collision with a lamp-post. (For sake of accuracy I may as well insert here my private source's stipulation that it *was not* a lamp-post at all, but a *telegraph pole*.) It is reasonable to suppose that instead of *two* cars at differing times ending hedgebound in the one instance and pole- or post-stricken in the second, thanks to the phantom playing the same trick *twice*, there was only *one* car – and that Mr Evans was behind its wheel. But an investigator can never be absolutely certain. A great deal would be answered if we were given the dates on which Mr Evans' dual-encounter took place. Such basic units of information would appear on the surface easily located; in practice they are as elusive as the Loch Ness Monster.

There are grounds for supposing that the car-crash portion of the story dates from some month in 1977[13] and that the more typical episode in which Mr Evans picked up a disappearing passenger was separated from it by no appreciable time-lag. The implication of the *Sunday Express* article was that both were recent; however, careful re-reading shows that this logic is founded upon the inference that national papers do not use 'old news' – that the events must have happened within days of being reported in print. In fact, it seems that this piece of Nunney news *was* old and given a certain freshness only by the activities of the Silver Jubilee ghost-hunters, which can be definitely pinned down to the first week of August 1977. Not only this; there has been the suggestion that the second instalment of the Evans story was staged as far back as March (1977), while the first – the more typical vanishing Hitch-Hiker effect – was remote from it by as much as *two years*.[14]

Impinging upon the problems of dating the Evans encounters are those relating to place: *where* are they supposed to have happened?

Analysing various treatments of the incidents in the regional press does not remedy that deficiency. Nor, on the strength of this material, does the ghost appear to obey the tenets of folklore, where spirits always confine their hauntings to well-circumscribed routes. The Nunney specimen seems to want to travel in either direction, Frome to Nunney or vice versa, according to some personal whim; in Royal and Girvan's version he is heading for yet another destination (Nunney Catch), while my private source disclosed that to Mr Evans he expressed the wish to ride to Badcox, the name given to a junction of eight roads in Frome itself – the opposite way entirely. Finally, the *Somerset Standard* referred to 'the ghost of Three Ponds Hill', a slight rise just after the straight stretch leading out of Nunney. One local resident, who will be properly introduced in a moment, agreed that this was thought

The entrance to the village of Nunney: another possible pick-up point for the Phantom Hitch-Hiker? (*photograph by Sheila Donaghy*)

to have been the site of the first incident.

The subsequent episode terminating with the car wrapped around a lamp-post/telegraph pole (or stuck in a hedge) *ought* to be identified with the same place, since we read that awareness of the Hitch-Hiker at the very locale where he had seen him before was the impetus for Mr Evans losing control of his vehicle. Unluckily, the *Bath and West Evening Chronicle* of 4 August 1977 tells it differently; the crash occurred near Frome. What was the Ghost of Three Ponds Hill doing so far from his usual pick-up point? The ultimate conclusion is that it is not only impossible for the incident(s) to be dated with any reliability: it is even debatable as to where it or they supposedly occurred.

What remains is a residue that would mollify few parapsychologists, who like their facts concise and beyond dispute. Somewhere along a three-mile length of road at some time between 1975-1977 Mr Evans claims to have picked up an undescribed male hitch-hiker who vanished – at a spot again left unspecified. On a second occasion, perhaps in 1977 (and certainly prior to August of that year), he saw the same presumed-apparition at a place perhaps, but not necessarily, identical with that of the former encounter and crashed because of it.

Had Mr Evans not gone to the police to file a report of that first incident – had the police not felt that report had something of truth about it – the sequel might have appeared a desperate excuse for dangerous driving. Here is a contradiction very similar to the one we saw emerging from the Montpellier case: regardless of flaws in the witness's story as it is related by the press, Mr Evans's actions in contacting the police about his incredible-sounding experience suggest he may genuinely have believed in the Phantom Hitch-Hiker. As police testimony indicates that he is not the only person to have proffered such an account to them, there is a further indication that other motorists have also shared that belief.

The Nunney vigilantes
The descriptive facts of the Evans double-encounter being so embroiled in contradiction, it is a relief to present a more decisive account of what really lay behind the Nunney Silver Jubilee Committee's ghost patrols. For if the Phantom Hitch-Hiker gains some credibility from the police-reported incidents and the Evans episodes, then his existence was considerably boosted by the unusual and newsworthy reactions of the Committee's organizers. Obscure as other aspects of the story may remain, a reader is inclined to think that if a sober, responsible body was moved to set up a ghost-watching rota, then assuredly something *very* serious was going on in this quiet corner of Somerset.

Mr Ron Macey appears to have been the fountain-head of many dramatic and entertaining quotes by means of which the regional and national presses gave readers to understand that Nunney's fund-raising events were in ghostly jeopardy. He is presented as co-ordinator of the patrols, a man who believed that the Committee had to find an answer to the mystery before the village's functions were even more seriously affected than they had been already; he was also the person whose tactical remark on reasoning with the ghost passed, via the *Bath and West Evening Chronicle*, into the columns of *The Weekly News*.[15]

The nature of the ghost patrols was a blend of the earnest and the light-hearted. Mervyn Hancock of the *Somerset Standard* went along with the vigilantes on the first of these fact-finding missions, which fell on Monday 1 August; a photographer was (somewhat optimistically) present to record any paraphysical event. But there was nothing to record, despite a member of the squad adopting what was intended as a deliberate 'come and get me' manner to provoke the phantom into appearing. The most significant thing that Mr Hancock noted was a 'spooky sound'. Mr Hillier claimed slightly more success for the hunters when he told the *Sunday Express* that (on a subsequent patrol, presumably) they met a couple who had seen a shadowy figure in the lane earlier that week. This was as close as the Nunney Silver Jubilee's Committee came to a supernatural phenomenon.

Mr Macey has now exchanged the house he occupied on the haunted road for a home in Cornwall, but when I set about researching the background to the Nunney vigilante patrols I was able to speak to a pair who were equally instrumental in putting the ghost patrols into operation. As a result of two telephone conversations the published story of these 'evidential' incidents can now be amended.

The best way to describe them came from Mr Fred L'Estrange, who acted as Chairman of the Silver Jubilee Committee at the time: 'purely a publicity gimmick'. As much might have been guessed when Mr Owen Hillier (whom we have already heard quoted by the newspapers) greeted my initial inquiry about the Nunney Hitch-Hiker with a hearty laugh. Quite simply, the Committee had decided to use the locally-known stories of the ghost as a means of publicizing the village's August Fair. 'It worked, actually,' put in Mr L'Estrange. They had patrolled 'to see what we could see', as Mr Hillier phrased it, and they certainly met the couple who had encountered a shadowy form as the press stated. But that was all. They had not expected to do more than stimulate some attention for the forthcoming attractions and in the light of what these gentlemen had to say the published articles on the vigilantes take on another perspective.

In particular, the comments of Mr Hillier were produced by the *Sunday Express* as implying that he was unable to escape the suspicion that someone or something might be behind him whenever he drove along the road at night – suggesting that he, too, believed in the ghost. Over the telephone he explained that he had travelled the road at all hours of the day and night without experiencing anything out of the ordinary and that he always attributed any 'funny sensations' to a prior awareness of the tales that it was haunted. Taken overall, the ghost-patrol aspects of the Nunney affair cannot be regarded as direct corroboration or evidence in favour of the Phantom Hitch-Hiker.

Yet taken obliquely, they *can*. The Nunney Silver Jubilee Committee did not *invent* the Phantom Hitch-Hiker, but adopted the locally-told (and believed?) tales of him to promote an unusual and effective kind of advertising; the ghost came first, the ghost patrols afterwards. I understand that it was the car accident 'a few months before' (says Mr L'Estrange) the August Fair that gave them the idea. In short, they were playing upon something that had already created an air of 'difference' about the village. Both men were emphatic that their plan was not intended to disparage what they had heard testified to as an authentic piece of apparitional phenomena. Anxious to avoid giving the impression that the Nunney ghost was a complete sham, Mr L'Estrange pointed out that there had been 'several' genuine reports made to the police and that the incident involving the car in the hedge – which, we have seen, constitutes one of the main articles of belief in the 1977 sightings – could be confirmed by a Nunney girl who had seen the out-of-place vehicle while walking with her boyfriend towards Frome. The driver, Mr L'Estrange added, 'was absolutely 100 per cent convinced' of the fact he had seen a man in the road; he was badly 'shaken up' and remained so for some days after. As for the supposed original of the apparition, he mentioned the deceased American serviceman of whom I had heard during my short visit to the village.

An inconclusive conclusion

The Phantom Hitch-Hiker of the Frome-Nunney Road is in many ways typical of its kind. Most readers and researchers become aware of it through the medium of the press, where it is rendered in a simple, almost ingenuous manner, with well-selected and occasionally mirth-provoking quotes from equally well-chosen, possibly influential persons. Closer scrutiny of the varying accounts then reveals not so much inaccuracies as changes of detail, and all too often contradictions. The parapsychologist who dares to tackle such a case will not find this state of affairs to his liking. For every fact that he manages to align with another, there will be a contradiction somewhere else; for every fact he manages to plug into gaps left by the printed accounts, there will be one that refuses to become involved. Small wonder incidents of this kind are usually left to folklorists.

The journalists were neither irresponsible nor deliberately misleading in their handling of the Nunney case; they merely responded in sharp fashion to what seemed a good news item with scope for touches of light comedy inbuilt: the ghost story as entertainment with a rural setting. The latter phase of the story features a purposeful (yet innocent) sham in which the 'vigilantes' exploited the ghost's publicity-value; far from driving people *away* from the village, it drew them *to* it. But it is important to remember that this and the less subtle horseplay that followed derived, however feebly, from what passed for an authentically paranormal phenomenon. These incidents comprise a body of ill-defined local traditions that tend to give the apparition a respectable vintage (and which can neither be decisively substantiated nor challenged) and a number of modern reports lacking certain desirable corroborative data, yet confirmed in the sense that the police testify to having received ostensibly truthful eye-witness statements of a Phantom Hitch-Hiker at large.

The Nunney case is a good illustration of how difficult it can be to disinter parapsychological fact from folklore's fiction, even assuming the former to be present at the outset. Many would *not* make that assumption, in spite of press and oral informants' assertions that it 'really happened'. It is easier – far easier – to rule that there is no unassailable evidence that the lane between Frome and Nunney was ever haunted in the way the reports stipulate.

We are left with the awkward question as to whether or not motorists would try to hoax the police with so unlikely a tale as that of a vanishing passenger. The Nunney affair certainly does not prove that the Phantom Hitch-Hiker 'exists'; but it may prove that a few people at least believe he does – some of them to the point where they put a report of the doubtful spectre before the authorities. Those readers charitable enough to accept that the witnesses may at any rate *think* they have met a hitch-hiking ghost will likely be speculating on probable sources that might be responsible for that illusion. Others will have reached the conclusion that some liars shamelessly resort to folklore for their fabrications. This dichotomy forms the topic of the following chapter.

FOUR: LIES AND MISTAKEN IDENTITIES

Some of the most highly-regarded ghost stories on record are based upon nothing more substantial than the unsupported testimony of a solitary witness – a person emotionally involved in the unusual events he or she is asking us to accept took place. The sceptic will say that this is precisely the weakness of psychical research: it is forced to put its faith in what people *say* they have experienced. Parapsychologists might retaliate by asserting that there have been enough cases where the witness established his/her credibility by reporting the alleged encounter immediately after it happened to one or more independent people, who thus serve as witnesses *after* the fact; or that there have also been incidents where an apparition was seen by two (or more) witnesses simultaneously. However, the hardened critic then explains the cases away as 'collective hallucinations' (which really explains nothing at all) or as collective hoaxes.

The Phantom Hitch-Hiker canon contains examples of both single-person and collectively-witnessed encounters. Inevitably, these are vulnerable to both types of dismissal. This is always supposing the researcher is lucky enough to pierce the traditional cloak of anonymity worn by the witness(es) to the story, or, by way of substitute, to trace some reliable person who has done so in his stead.

Evaluation of testimony: techniques and limitations

There is no objective proof that the most outwardly-credible of ghost-seers is *not* lying about his or her experience. The statistics of probability scarcely apply to ghostly encounters; the situation confronting the investigator is not like calculating the odds against dealing four people identical hands at bridge. And contrary to popular conception, there are no mechanical/ technological, chemical or psychological techniques that can be relied upon to secure the plain, unvarnished truth. Even where it is possible and ethical to use them, as hypnosis has been used to probe the memories of persons who have been victims of witnesses of crimes *and* those of the people who claim to have been abducted by aliens from space, their introduction may only complicate the issue at hand. For these and other reasons, psychical researchers tend to rely, as they have always done, upon personal interviews with witnesses and thence upon good, old-fashioned character assessment.

Some people can lie persistently and fluently – and con-vincingly. Parapsychology has suffered from a few of their number in the past, and will no doubt do so again. The most common motivation involves the lie told to flatter the ego – to make the teller more important, the centre of the attention – or perhaps the kind designed for the dubious delight of 'putting one over on the experts'. Investigators of the paranormal will always be on the look-out for warnings that both or either are in operation. Again, not all 'ghostly lies' are born of deep-seated motives. There are many social situations when ghost stories are invented (or re-invented) purely to conform with the topic of conversation; the fabricator contributes partly from the desire to impress, partly to be sociable. It is not impossible to lie successfully to a psychical researcher, but it is not easy, either, because he or she is liable to ask too many questions and follow up on contradictions. The researcher may even ask the 'witness' to put the account in writing and sign it. In short, the researcher does not approach the story in the spirit of entertain-ment or sociability but in a businesslike, scientific fashion, which imposes great strain on the fabricator's resolve to keep the fabrication going.

The actual manner in which a story is told – the narrative style, not the contents themselves – can provide a measure of reliability. A story told flatly, matter-of-factly or hesitantly is more convincing than one accompanied by facial gynastics, assumed 'character' accents, attempts at dramatic voice modulations and select Gothic diction of the 'To my utmost horror, my startled gaze perceived' order. This is not to say that the account must be vernacular and incoherent, but essays at 'professionalism' are decidedly suspect. Study of the circum-stances under which the relation takes place can assist; if the witness came forward reluctantly or was discovered by accident and talks with evident or incipient signs of fearing ridicule, that person is less likely to be seeking self-publicity.

Most researchers want to hear the witness give the account more than once. By the second time around a parapsychologist may have formed an opinion of the witness's health and mental faculties. The relevance of psychological factors like memory flaws, as shown in embellishments, exaggerations or inconsistencies registered over the two tellings of the story, the person's susceptibility to expectancy, auto- or external sources of suggestion, preconceived ideas on the paranormal and even self-delusions may have emerged. Any or all of these may detract to a greater or lesser degree from the credibility of a story; few accounts are devoid of any traces whatsoever of these things. But when all other forms of independent corroboration are missing (as must be the case in single-person testimonies) the cautious investigator may weigh the above considerations and then concede the witness is not fabricating. This concession is not the same as professing a belief in ghosts, nor that in this instance there was one there for the witness to see: it simply means that the investigator is prepared to believe that the witness may have *thought* he saw one. Short of coming upon an apparitional experience that was filmed as it took place, we can hardly ask for much more than that.

Having evaluated the witness, the researcher will proceed to evaluate features of the story itself. Through familiarity with the literature extant on the subject – and good researchers *will* be reasonably well-read within their own subject-area – it can be established very generally what a spontaneous case will 'sound like'. Its sheer incredibility is no deterrent; because a story sounds incredible does not mean it is not true, since psychical research is largely the sum of incredible-sounding stories. It may be reassuring if the phenomena described correspond with those in cases already written of in the literature, but departures from the paranormal norm cannot be ruled out; we know too little about anomalous phenomena to be able to pronounce with confidence on what may or may not be possible. Even so, as C. G. Jung wrote:

In most cases their authenticity is confirmed not only by the freedom with which they were reported, but also by independent parallel stories. Since it cannot be doubted that such reports are found at all times and places, there is no sufficient reason for doubting the veracity of individual reports.[1]

Folklorists will retort that the ubiquity of a story like the Phantom Hitch-Hiker proves only how widely it has been disseminated and relocated. It is when the ghost fails to observe the conventions of the motif with which it is associated that the issue becomes more complex than folklore leads us to believe.

A handful of modern Hitch-Hikers diverge from the pattern whereby the ghost provides evidence of its co-identity with a tragically-killed person. In their inconclusiveness, their purposelessness, they move closer to the authenticated apparitions known to parapsychology, where ghosts seldom show any interest in the disclosure of unpunished crimes, the whereabouts of buried treasure or any of the motivations that obsess them in folk-fiction. We are not given neatly-rounded accounts that follow the classic tripartite division of beginning, middle and end; like the typical apparitions in the Society for Psychical Research's records, they pose as simple actors in single episodes, isolated units that defy our ideas on artistic or narrative balance.

Again related to the manner of telling are the narrative details: presence or absence of artificial colouring, scene-setting by use of supposedly atmospheric effects, and all the rest. Though the fiction-merchant may suppose that details like the 'bloodstain over the heart' add a touch of realism, they do the reverse; nor do Gothic touches like cemeteries and ruined houses figure very strongly in veridical ghost stories. They are complications – over-elaborations that attempt to conform to a received and traditional standard of what ghost stories should be like. Since a 'good' ghost story is far harder to construct than most people realize, the fabricator is inclined to over-do the stage-props – the scenic details especially – and to underscore the ending. In most bad ghost stories the nature of the ghost is not left to inference but is baldly stated. In all respects, the maker-up of 'true' ghost stories is prone to do too much.

A ride to the cemetery

All but a few Phantom Hitch-Hiker stories fail for one or more of the reasons just given. Any survey or appeal for personal experiences relating to ghosts is likely to attract a few Hitch-Hiker accounts of this fiction-ill-disguised-as-fact variety. An invitation to readers by the Swiss magazine *Schweizerischer Beobachter* netted psychologist Aniela Jaffé over 1200 letters containing about 1500 accounts, which she analyzed in her *Apparitions and Precognition* (1963), a study of Jungian archetypes within such experiences. There was only one Phantom Hitch-Hiker, and the writer awarded it a chapter of its own – not because of its realistic qualities, but for exactly the opposite reason.[2]

'Drive me past the cemetery' is fairly obviously what Beardsley and Hankey would term a Version C story, for the girl is not met by the roadside but in a place of entertainment – a restaurant somewhere in the Far East. There are plenty of details: the nervous young lady spills wine on her white dress, tells the witnesses where she lives yet insists on being driven past the cemetery, which is in the opposite direction. The two witnesses lose her after she alights at this spot. Next day they call at the girl's home and identify her from a photograph. She died in an accident two years previously and the evening before had been the anniversary of this unhappy event. As if this were not enough, the parents have the grave opened, thus revealing the girl's undecayed body (suggestive of the vampire legend) with a wine-stain on her dress and mud on her shoes.

Ms Jaffé almost refuses to comment on this story. To her, it is devoid of significant, symbolic data and the style contrasts with the plain, monotonous tone of the other material she quotes. *'The lack of archetypal features seems to be a criterion of the improbability of the "experience"'* – the italics are hers. Another way of saying this might be to describe the thing as too artificial, too much so to even approximate the sort of account readers might concede to be veridical. There is a clear credibility gap, then, between the artistically-devised 'true story', which is fiction, and the real life experience it attempts to mimic.

The rare Phantom Hitch-Hiker stories free from over-attention to artifice may resemble authenticated apparitional events only by accident. Alternatively, they do not have to be outright lies; charitably-minded readers may like to hazard that they represent delusions of some kind, spurious phenomena where the witness's sensory apparatus – hindered, reduced, devaluated by nocturnal conditions and the motion of the vehicle, perhaps – has fallen short rather than his or her moral fibre. 'For the night beguileth men's eyes,' wrote Lewes Lavater in the third chapter of his *Of Ghostes and Spirites walking by Night* (1572), 'And therefore none ought to marvel, if travellers towards night or at midnight, mistake stones, trees, stubs or such like to be sprites and elves.'

One can only say that if events took place strictly as described, then the Phantom Hitch-Hiker sounds too detailed and prolonged an experience to permit this kind of interpretation. People may sometimes mistake roadside trees or posts for human figures, may stop their cars to offer them a lift, but once the optical illusion is recognized as such the motorist does not then invite the post or tree into the car. It is more reasonable to speculate that such natural objects serve as the stimulus for a hallucination, though it is less easy to produce evidence supporting that speculation.

That nocturnal motorists not infrequently mistake half-seen natural objects for *super*natural ones is indisputable. A vivid example took place in my own area of Thurrock (Essex) in 1977, when two eighteen-year-olds driving home early one Sunday morning sighted a ghostly tableau of monkishly-cowled figures posed in a country lane. For the shocked witnesses this macabre scene was beyond all logical explanation.

Only some days later was it announced that the 'ghosts' were three young men pausing for a rest while walking the last few miles between the nearest railway station and their homes, their heads and upper bodies swaddled against the drizzle with towels and squash-shirts. Perhaps we could not expect a

The Ghosts pose for the *Gazette*. Photographer David Henderson recreates the late-night scene in which three Ockendon youths were mistaken for supernatural beings by a pair of passing motorists. (*photograph courtesy of the Thurrock Gazette*)

night-motorist to make an accurate assessment of such a spectacle rushing at him without warning; equally significant, had the young men not come forward the incident would have remained a convincing road-ghost case.[3]

Perhaps the victims of this illusion were conditioned or influenced by subconscious recollection of late-night horror films. Some form of received impression or interpretation may have contributed to the panic of insurance-brokers Barry Collings and Steven Pope six months later when they stopped to offer a lift to an attractive blonde in a dishevelled white evening dress on the A229 (Kent) opposite the Veglios Motel. She did not reply – merely smiled – and the two witnesses noticed that the blustery night had no effect on her loose, fair hair; everything about her seemed curiously still. Concluding that the young lady was not of this world, Mr Pope promptly accelerated away. The most interesting point here is the way that, despite the fact the event occurred close to Maidstone, some way to the south of Blue Bell Hill, journalists raced to tie it in with the Phantom Hitch-Hiker who reputedly haunts that locality.[4] Eye-witnesses' feelings to the contrary, many critics would have no trouble in disregarding the detail about the girl's abnormally wind-resistant coiffure or the suggestion that she was other than human on the grounds that the men's imagination (disturbed, let us say, by the unusual setting) ran away with them. Always supposing, of course, the critics would admit that the encounter happened at all. One can only fantasize about what might have befallen had the uncanny blonde accepted the offer of a ride with Messrs. Pope and Collings.

The ill-tempered traveller

With the possibility that chance conditions may conspire to transform an ordinary person at the roadside into a passable imitation of a ghost, we can review the strange if not lunatic behaviour of the Man in the Mackintosh, who may be categorized as both Phantom Hitch-Hiker and Vanishing Accident Casualty. His story is found in at least three sources, although 'Terror of the Phantom Hitch-Hiker' (*Weekend*, 28 September-4 October 1977) is really Peter Moss's précis of his own treatment of a lorry driver's experiences on the infamous A38 near Wellington in *Ghosts Over England*.[5] Combining this with material from Andrew Green's *Our Haunted Kingdom*, a mini-history of the Man in the Mac (or perhaps it should be Overcoat) can be assembled as follows.

Southwest of Taunton the A38 bends down to Wellington and passes through the village of Rumwell. Ignoring the ten accident reports mentioned in passing by Mr Green for the period 1968-1973, it is in this locality that the first printed witness account of the car-careless apparition is set.[6] According to the *Western Morning News* in August 1970, Mrs Swithenbank from North Street, Taunton swerved to avoid a middle-aged man in a long grey coat who was straddling the centre of the road near Heatherton Grange Hotel; when she decided to give him a piece of her mind, she found he had vanished.[7] Publication of this account was sufficient to encourage two other motorists to relate similar tales of sightings and prompt evasive action, while an identical-sounding situation caused a motorcyclist to fall from his machine and break a limb at White Ball, four miles to the west. Still at White Ball, another driver got a rare glimpse of the phantom's face in profile; the sources state or imply that in other instances the face of the 'man' was averted. As a result of these 1970 reports it was possible to gather that a middle-aged male apparition in a long grey coat or mackintosh – perhaps, on the strength of Mrs Swithenbank's account, also carrying a torch – was believed to be active around this section of the A38, inviting or daring collisions with oncoming traffic.

This phenomenon was thought by an Exeter long-distance lorry driver named Harold Unsworth to be the key to a mystery he had concealed for twelve years – from fear of ridicule *and* because of his own reluctance to believe what had happened to him. In 1958 he had met the Man in a Mackintosh not once but several times and these encounters were now set down (1970) in the *Exeter Express and Echo*.[8]

On the first occasion he was returning through foul weather to his Cullompton depot at 3 a.m. when he took pity on a middle-aged man in a cream or grey mac who waited, torch in hand, bedraggled and hatless, near the Blackbird Inn, one mile west of Heatherton Grange on the A38. In a voice described as 'well-educated', the sodden stranger asked to be dropped at Beam Bridge by the Holcombe Rogus crossroads and spent part of the four-mile ride regaling a slightly uneasy Mr Unsworth with circumstantial and ghastly tales of how many accidents had occurred during the week. The driver was not sorry to part company with him.

The atmospheric details of the late hour and bad weather became a constant throughout Mr Unsworth's acquaintanceship with the peculiar passenger. The situation was repeated only a few days later, and then after an interval of one month. Considering the man's curious habit of wandering with a torch along the A38 in the dead of night and pouring rain, not to mention his unsavoury choice of conversational topics, Mr Unsworth began to think the fellow might be mentally deficient. But it was not until November 1958 that the lorry-driver's own mental equilibrium was even more seriously assaulted.

The rain was heavy, the hour late . . . the man wanted to go to Beam Bridge as usual. But once there he asked Mr Unsworth to wait, since he needed to collect some cases and to be taken further up the road. Mr Unsworth *did* wait: he waited twenty minutes and then gave up. Near a transport café three miles along the road he saw a frantically-waved torch which he interpreted as perhaps a distress signal from some fellow-motorist in trouble – until his headlights picked out the familiar figure in a mackintosh . . .

No vehicle had come along the road in either direction and Mr Unsworth's sense of alarm did not dispose him to pick up a hitch-hiker who could cover such a distance in so short a time-span. Trying not to look at the Hitch-Hiker he began to pull out, only to have the man hurl himself in front of the lorry. Collision was unavoidable; there ought to have been the impact of body on metal, but there was not. Applying his brakes, Mr Unsworth brought the lorry to a halt a few dozen yards further on before jumping from the cab. There in the middle of the road was the Man in a Mackintosh, shaking a fist and cursing at having been ignored. It was at this dramatic moment that he turned his back and vanished instantly. Mr Unsworth also vanished: he drove away from the scene as fast as possible.

Analysis of Mr Unsworth's story focuses upon two possibly inexplicable factors. The man's persistent presence on the A38 at such an early hour and in such inclement weather, or his gloomy conversations are not among them; these things may appear odd or unlikely, but they are not beyond the realms of normality. It may be significant that at a later stage in the proceedings the lorry-driver considered that his passenger might be mentally ill – a part-explanation that could perhaps inject some meaning into the man's choice of travelling times – yet even so Mr Unsworth continued to give him lifts. Up until the final meeting the behaviour of the Man in a Mackintosh was perplexing, even disturbing, yet not of a sort to cause the witness to regard it as evidence of the supernatural. The two elements that may be put forward to suggest that the hitch-hiker was some kind of apparitional entity are: (a) the appearance of the Hitch-Hiker three miles down the road from where Mr Unsworth had dropped him twenty minutes previously. Both the amount of time and distance depend on estimations from a witness who is telling his story twelve years after it took place.

While there is an unfairly underrated argument that such time-lags between occurrences and tellings tend to *diminish* rather than embellish striking ('paranormal') elements in an account, it is reasonable to be cautious about the total accuracy of details in a narrative told so long after the event. If we wish to see the Man in a Mackintosh as an ordinary human, though, we shall have to confess that he made very good time through the rain to cover the distance to where Mr Unsworth next saw him. Four miles an hour is a good walking speed in fair weather conditions; the Hitch-Hiker did rather better than that. But, as just mentioned, for this factor to be evidential or inexplicable within our terms of reference it would have to be shown beyond all doubt that Mr Unsworth's estimates of time (twenty minutes) and distance (three miles) were impeccable.

But taken as written, (b) the man's survival of a collision with a moving lorry and his vanishing thereafter seem to be outside rational explanation. Even allowing for the possibility – not a very strong one – that the man only *seemed* to leap into the lorry's path, baulking or drawing back at the last minute, perhaps, and in a manner that Mr Unsworth, high up in the driver's cab, was prevented from seeing clearly, there is the man's abrupt disappearance to explain. This last phase in the manifestations brings the case into conformity with the experiences of the other A38 motorists who hit, or almost hit, a pedestrian who vanished when they stopped to investigate. It is noteworthy that, after behaving reasonably well during his free rides, the Man in the Mackintosh reverted to this practice only when it seemed that Mr Unsworth was for once *not* about to offer him a lift. The post-collision disappearance might almost imply an infuriated response to the fact that he was being ignored – as indeed other drivers, intent on their journeys, had been oblivious to his 'existence' till the man materialized in front of their vehicles.

A sceptic could aver that there is absolutely no substantiating evidence that Mr Unsworth ever knew the Hitch-Hiker before the Exeter press promoted the story. Reading all these A38 ghost stories in the newspapers, he may have decided to become a contributor to the round. Another possibility is that the testimonies of the other motorists affected his memory of the 1958 sequence of events – a sequence he had failed to make sense of over the twelve years separating them from the new spate of tales. At some point did Mr Unsworth's recollections of the mysterious hitch-hiker begin to conform with, or begin to be coloured by, what he had read in the papers? Did the stories of the vanishing man in the road lend themselves to his own experience of a suspiciously weird yet otherwise normal man whose final appearance became, in the witness's mind, so confused with the 1970 accounts that it suddenly seemed supernatural? The theme of mistaken identity, with the Man in a Mackintosh being a real person interpreted (at a late stage) as a ghostly being, is bedevilled by the culminating fact that, before the lorry-driver's eyes, he *vanished*. Human hitch-hikers cannot *do* that.

We can only hypothesize that *if* the man *was* an ordinary human, his sinister behaviour in unusual, isolated surroundings *may* have had an oppressive effect upon Mr Unsworth, who finally reacted to the barely conscious psychological pressure by hallucinating the last part of his experience, notably the collision and disappearance. But there are said to have been several such experiences; this A38 case-collation lists at least five instances in 1970 or thereabouts when drivers were forced to take emergency action because of the apparition, which subsequently vanished from the road. In fact, there have been more reports of this inconclusive type in Britain than there have been of typical Phantom Hitch-Hikers. This revives an intriguing question which must be taken up later: if these experiences are purely hallucinatory, why are so many people experiencing the same kind of hallucination?

By way of an appendix, aspects of the Unsworth case can be compared with another ambiguous incident, which may or may not have been fictive, set once more in the pouring rain but on this occasion near California's San Bernadino Mountains and with a carload of churchbound teenagers as witnesses. They passed a hitch-hiker; a mile further on they passed him again. After a third sighting of this speedy traveller their engine showed signs of malfunction and they turned back. No cars had overtaken them but the man on the road had now gone, nor was there any conceivable place where he could have hidden himself. The boys believed the Hitch-Hiker to have been a heaven-sent messenger warning them of danger in the mountains ahead. A correspondent who sent this story to the *Los Angeles Mirror and Daily News* (2 April 1955) swore to the honesty and reliability of the witnesses, but columnist Matt Weinstock preferred to believe the tale was 'pure folklore'.[9]

Persons unknown? The guitarist's adventure

The vanishing of a passenger before a witness's very eyes is difficult to rationalize away; even when those eyes were not constantly upon the Hitch-Hiker, it is hard to explain how he/she disappears from inside a moving vehicle or (in the case of a pseudo-traffic accident casualty) its immediate vicinity. This insubstantial quality is of course shared by both the ghosts of folk-fiction and the authenticated apparitions known to parapsychology.

By definition, an urban legend is a widely-told, widely-believed tale resting on apocryphal (non-existent) evidence. The Mouse in a Coke Bottle is fairly representative: perturbed by the unpalatable flavour of his/her soft drink, the witness-victim discovers a whole or partial mouse in the bottle and successfully sues the drink company for thousands of dollars. Yet, occasionally urban legends have been known to come true. Professor Brunvand has suggested that in the fortunately rare cases where rodents have unquestionably been found in soft drinks, the incident may reveal that life has been assisted in mimicking art – by the adroit fingers of some practical jokers who appreciate the fun-potential of the urban legend. And if there are people who will use the Mouse in a Coke Bottle motif as inspiration for a practical joke, might there not be others who will borrow the Vanishing Hitch-Hiker – a classic within the urban legend genre?

It seems hard for a practical joker who is not also a stuntman/stuntwoman or escapologist to exit safely and imperceptibly from an automobile in motion; harder, one might imagine, than to insert a dead mouse into a firmly-sealed coke bottle without leaving tell-tale traces. But a borrowed coat or sweater draped on a pre-selected grave as per C-Variant Hitch-Hiker tales might not present much difficulty. Professor Brunvand muses that this may have occurred, raising 'the interesting possibility of hitchhiking-ghost hoaxes, based on the plot of the popular urban legend'.[10]

A hoax in highly questionable taste, perhaps, but also a theory worth remembering when reading an account like that printed in the now defunct weekly magazine *Reveille* of 9 May 1975.[11] This tells how Richard Studholme, lead guitarist in the pop group Chicory Tip, interrupted his homeward journey through Kent to pick up a girl (undescribed) on 'Blueberry' (i.e. Blue Bell) Hill.[12] After the girl's case was stored in the car she asked to be taken to West Kingsdown but also requested Mr Studholme to call on her parents at Swanley after he dropped her off. She said little during the ride and the reader is left uninformed as to the message (if any) the guitarist was to convey. Having deposited the girl as arranged, Mr Studholme continued to the Swanley address where (as we might have anticipated) he found a bereaved parent who told him that his daughter had been killed two years before on the very spot at which the Hitch-Hiker had been waiting.

We are led to believe that Mr Studholme only reached the conclusion that his passenger had been a ghost after reading of another Blue Bell Hill motorist's collision with a girl whose body vanished before the police arrived. This could only be the heavily-publicized Maurice Goodenough episode (July 1974); the inference is that Mr Studholme's experience predated it, though it seems puzzling that his account did not appear in *Reveille* until ten months afterwards (May 1975). The fact that his girlfriend's brother was on the local police force (precisely where is not stated, nor whether he was involved in the hunt for the missing traffic accident victim) doubtless encouraged the pop star to accept that the Goodenough case was authentic. At this juncture he began to reassess his *own* nocturnal experience on the haunted hill.

The guitarist's initial reaction infuses an unexpected note of originality into what otherwise sounds a rather stereotyped tale. Not the shock, horror or deeply adverse response character-istic of the folk-tale witness on being told his passenger had been dead for some time before he met her as a Hitch-Hiker: Mr Studholme sensibly opted for a more logical solution, believing himself to have been the victim of a cruel hoax. The girl was, he supposed, a human with a warped sense of humour; she deliberately sent him off to an address where, as she knew, a family had lost a daughter some while before. So things may have remained, but on reading reports in the local papers following the Goodenough incident, he found that other drivers had undergone strange experiences on Blue Bell Hill . . .

Now Mr Studholme began to re-evaluate *his* experience, wondering whether he, too, was one of the select band to have encountered the Phantom Hitch-Hiker. And yet (as far as can be gathered from the article) his mind never rejected its first impressions about the normality of the incident; he had touched the girl, felt the suitcase – which presumably she took with her when they reached West Kingsdown – and, probably influenced a little by received opinions on paranormal effects, he mentions specifically that he felt no sensation of coldness during the drive. If we persist in maintaining that the witness's early assessment of the event was accurate – that the Hitch-Hiker was a cruel female hoaxer whose motives were and must remain obscure – we may be unmoved by the journalist's attempt to reinforce the 'supernatural' element in the traditional way, i.e., the assertion that other motorists had undergone this same experience, even down to calling on the bereaved parents at Swanley; unmoved, too, by the way he does not hesitate to align these events with the baffling case of the Goodenough 'accident'.

I leave it to the reader to decide whether Mr Studholme's first and more rationalistic assessment (a hoax) was more accurate than the second (a ghost), or indeed whether such an astounding tale told in the pages of a popular magazine deserves to be taken as read. But before anyone rejects the story out of hand as being too close to Beardsley and Hankey's C-Version Hitch-Hikers for comfort or credibility, it might be worth mentioning that in the absence of the witness himself (he is now resident in the USA) I contacted a person close to Mr Studholme for confirmation of the *Reveille* article. I was assured the incident *had* taken place as stated and (as someone once said of the young man who narrated the tale of the Stanbridge Hitch-Hiker which opened Chapter One), '"he's not the sort of person to make up something like that"'.

It is normally considered unacceptable for researchers to offer character-witness statements in lieu of more reliable evidence. Of prime value is first-hand testimony – the investigator's report of an interview, not with a friend of a friend of the witness, nor with his sister or his bank manager, but taken from the lips of that witness in person. It is almost axiomatic that where Phantom Hitch-Hikers are concerned one never receives this opportunity: the witness is traditionally anonymous, customarily unavailable.

It would therefore be a useful thing to track down and interview someone who abandoned such privileges and openly claimed to have had the experience of driving with a hitch-hiker who made a wholly unannounced disppearance in transit. According to the *Sunday Express* of 21 October 1979, carpet-fitter Roy Fulton of Dunstable was just such a person.

FIVE: ROY FULTON MEETS THE PHANTOM HITCH-HIKER

Roy Fulton is a slim, sandy-haired young man whose main leisure interests revolve around darts and Liverpool Football Club. He has no preoccupations whatsoever with occultism or the paranormal. However, it is not necessary to hold some prior belief in apparitions in order to see one, and Mr Fulton has gone on record as saying that he recently encountered one of the most disputed of them all: the hopelessly hackneyed Phantom Hitch-Hiker.

Night ride

As I said, you know, I was playing in a darts match over Leighton Buzzard; I left there about twenty past nine and I was driving through Stanbridge . . . and there's a road down there called Peddar's Lane . . . about 100 yards past there the street lights finish. There was a figure I [saw] on the left-hand side, thumbing a lift down there. I pulled up in front of him, so I could see him walking back into the headlights.

He had a dark-coloured jumper on, dark-coloured trousers, with an open white-collared shirt. He came up to the motor; he got in there and sat down – he even opened the door himself, I had nothing to do with opening the door. I asked him where he was going and he just pointed up the road – never said a word. So I assumed he was either going to Dunstable or Totternhoe.

So I was driving up the road, I suppose I was driving for – what, four, five or six minutes, I suppose, doing a speed of about 40 minimum.

I turned round to offer him a cigarette and the bloke had disappeared.

I braked, had a quick look in the back to see if he was there. He *wasn't* and I just gripped the wheel and drove like hell. And that's all – you know . . .

That's all: some would say it was too much. The passage just quoted is taken from a taped interview I had with Mr Fulton in early 1980; three years further on he was still maintaining that his story is authentic – that one dark October evening he *did* meet a Phantom Hitch-Hiker. I have played my tape to many people: to a handful of parapsychologists, to groups of school-children, to friends – to anyone who cared to listen. Naturally, their responses varied; one member of the Society for Psychical Research referred to it as a 'typical case of apparition', while a fourteen-year-old boy gave a tight-lipped sneer of, 'Nah, don't believe it'. Who is to say which is the more accurate evaluation? Common sense and folklorist concensus inclines towards the fourteen-year-old's assessment of the matter; parapsychologists who wish to vote on this side, though, are honour-bound to present good, logical reasons for doing so. Those reasons can only emerge after a thorough sifting of the evidence on offer.

Although Sally Staples was the first to turn Roy Fulton's allegations into national news with her *Sunday Express* article, 'Was it a Ghost that hitched a lift and . . .?' of 21 October 1979, it appears that the author of the original printed source was closer to the scene of the incident: Mrs Anne Cox (then Court), who described it in the *Dunstable Gazette* three days earlier.[1] By talking to her I obtained independent impressions of the case and of the eyewitness, as well as clarification on particular points left unanswered after my own conversation with him.

Establishing how this type of account first came to the ears of a journalist can prove a helpful guide in assessing its veracity. A ghost-seer who contacts a paper may be motivated by a genuine desire to relate a true experience, but they can also be inspired by the possibility of personal glory (or notoriety), if not by the idea of more tangible (financial) rewards. Neither form of aggrandisement – psychological or financial – necessarily proves the story to be a piece of fiction, but the mere fact that such a motive exists (or is firmly suspected to exist) *can* undermine the credibility of some cases as far as many investigators are concerned.

However, it appears that Roy Fulton did not make any such approach; Mrs Cox came across the story in a roundabout way, through the husband of a friend of the witness's wife. The issue of the *Dunstable Gazette* that included the 'Night Ride Riddle' appeared on a Thursday; next morning the *Sunday Express* telephoned the paper asking for further information. Certain embellishments to the story that appeared in the *Express's* treatment of the incident but were not in the *Dunstable Gazette's* preceding account – the local geography, the weather conditions, and so on – were thus provided by Anne Cox, who also passed on the names of two persons quoted with great effect in Sally Staples's write-up of the case: Mr Bill Stone, the publican, and Police Inspector Rowland.

Dwelling upon the way in which Roy Fulton's experience

became, in a sense, national property reveals how circumstantial details not found in the local paper's account were made available for the wider audience of the *Express*; more important, it may offer an answer to a puzzling discrepancy between the tale as told by Ms Staples and the testimony of the witness as recorded by myself on tape. I will point out the nature of this discrepancy and the possible solution to it presently. For what it may be worth, I can say that Roy Fulton did not strike me as a glory-seeker. '"Are you a star now?"' asked the pub's landlord Bill Stone, as he passed by with a swift glance at my whirring cassette recorder. '"*Yeah!*"' replied Roy in a tone that carried more than a hint of self-derision.

Or perhaps, the knowing sceptic will reply, the derision was aimed at the so-called investigator beside him. It goes without saying that 98 per cent of what follows rests solely on the unsupported word of a solitary witness who testifies to a 'truth' that bears a terrible resemblance to folklore – in which eventuality there are no means known to science to eliminate the possibility of a hoax. The remaining 2 per cent consists of the fact I found only minor and explicable inconsistencies between printed and oral (taped) versions of the story; the fact that Anne Cox was prepared to believe the man was telling the truth as he perceived it to be (her only doubts centering not on the integral points of the story but on a supposedly related 'historical' exegis to be discussed later); the equally-trusting reaction of the police; and lastly, the corporate acceptance of the tale among Roy's circle of acquaintances (which I had to take on trust), excepting perhaps one fellow who 'wouldn't believe it unless it happened to him'. If these indicators are not sufficient to sway the reader's judgement, the only feasible alternative is to think the incident a complete fabrication.

'"You look as if you'd just seen a ghost".'

Roy Fulton's account opens with him driving home from a darts match in Leighton Buzzard. Anyone who knows anything about darts matches (and more especially about the ambiance in which they are played) might infer that the witness had been imbibing pretty freely during that contest, but they would be wrong. The *Sunday Express* asserted that Roy had drunk one and a half pints of lager that evening; during our interview he amended the quantity to two pints and in addition gave me the impression that he is capable of taking that amount (and more) without losing touch with reality. Mr Fulton had good reason to be careful where alcohol was concerned. A carpet-fitter needs to be mobile – or as Roy himself puts it, his driver's licence is his job – and the Leighton Buzzard police are, he assured me, notoriously hard on drinking and driving offenders.

In sum, Roy Fulton denies he was drunk, or anywhere approaching drunk, on 12 October 1979. There was corroboration of this in what the Dunstable Police told me; as far as they could discern, Mr Fulton had been sober when he made his report. Besides, it is hard to see how two pints of lager (to take the outside figure) could have played a part in his experience. Can such a quantity induce *any* sort of alcoholic hallucination in a person, let alone one of vanishing hitch-hikers? This may not preclude the possibility that Roy Fulton's passenger may have been a hallucination of some other variety, but that is a complication which I do not wish to introduce at this time.

About one and a half miles west of the A5 lies the village of Stanbridge. Just past the Five Bells public house, and not far from where the lighting ends, Peddars Lane becomes Station Road. Anne Cox described the scene for me as 'quite an eerie sort of place, quite desolate and flat – one of those roads that go from one village to another. But it's a very flat sort of area; there's certainly no hills, no trenches, nor any trees to hide behind.'[2] It was here that Roy Fulton picked up his Phantom Hitch-Hiker.

He drove down the unlit stretch of road in his Mini van, not especially excited or nervous – certainly not thinking about ghosts, a topic which he confirmed (in response to my query) had not been discussed in the pub beforehand. There was no car radio to distract him. The night, 'as black as it would have got', was broached by occasional fog patches: 'that's what made it more spooky than anything'. Then he saw the Hitch-Hiker.

I asked Roy to confirm that his first impression had been of a man soliciting a ride like any ordinary hitcher. His answer was:

Yeah! He was thumbing a lift, you know, standing sort of square on with his thumb out in the road. I pulled over in front of him, so that he had to walk back [i.e., towards] the motor.

For an interval of several seconds, then, the witness had the man in the clear view of his headlights; he could pick out the dark hair, white shirt, dark trousers. The only peculiar and perhaps disturbing element about what he saw was the man's face: very pale and unusually long, which Roy indicated for me by tracing an imaginary continuation to his own jawline. He was, moreover, totally real and ostensibly solid to Roy's eyes: 'I saw him as clearly as I can see you,' he expostulated.

Next, we note that it is the Hitch-Hiker who takes the initiative, not the driver: he walks back to the waiting car and *opens the door*.

Here is the only discrepancy of any significance appearing between my recorded and printed sources, for whereas the *Sunday Express* says that Roy was the one who let the Hitch-Hiker into the van there is his taped statement that he 'had nothing to do with opening the door'. I heard him repeat this several times and have the feeling that the contradiction came about as a result of journalistic inference. Sally Staples wrote her account from information provided by Anne Cox, whose *Dunstable Gazette* piece does not specify *who* opened the car door. It is likely that attribution of this action to the driver was a piece of logical deduction on the part of the *Express* writer. Conscious that a ghost story was being told, uncertain as to who made it possible for the Hitch-Hiker to get into the vehicle and supposing apparitions incapable of such physical effects as manipulating door handle mechanisms, the writer may have concluded that it had to be Roy Fulton who was responsible for this phase of the event.

The fact that the opening of the door had the proper result of activating the car's interior lighting adds credibility to the picture created by Roy Fulton; the next stage, however, may impress some readers as being somewhat unlikely, if not downright unbelievable. When asked where he wants to go, the hitcher points wordlessly in a direction which could mean Dunstable or Totternhoe. There is no conversation; the entire episode is noiseless save (presumably) for the purr of the car's engine, without even a rustle of clothing. Surely a motorist in this uneasy situation would make *some* attempt to communicate with his passenger?

Eventually Roy Fulton *did* make such an attempt; he offered the man beside him a cigarette, a small enough act but one which effectively interrupted the silence that accompanied the arrival of the hitch-hiker. More significant, it was the crucial action that alerted the motorist to the sudden absence of his short-term companion.

Before we move on to this event, two points can be made. The first is a generalization; sympathetic readers may take the ostensible unreality of the silent drive as an argument in favour of its *reality*. If Roy Fulton had decided to 'fake up' a ghost story, he would perhaps have tried to emphasize the initial credibility of his phantom by producing a talking specimen conforming to our expectations – especially our expectations concerning Hitch-Hikers, which (as Chapter Two indicated) are usually very vocal. And why not also conform with established folklore precedent by picking up a female Hitch-Hiker rather than a male one?

The second point is more specific. While we may find it strange that the witness did not try to engage the hitcher in conversation, we should respect the fact that Mr Fulton did *not* regard it so at the time. During our interview he admitted that the man's silence *had* struck him as slightly unusual, but any incipient alarm he may have felt was overcome by the rationalization that the dark-haired stranger might have been deaf and dumb. That, he insisted, was just his interpretation. Apart from this, Roy is neither given to long conversations with total strangers nor is he the type of person to force conversation upon a companion who patently does not feel like talking. On reflection, the lack of exchange between driver and Hitch-Hiker may not be notably suspect, whereas a talking ghost might have been uncomfortably close to folklore.

The uncommunicative nature of the passenger makes intelligible the next part of the story. Roy drives off, confining his attention to the road, not glancing at the person beside him:

The interior light came on, I remember that; the interior light came on, the car door shut . . . that is the last – I'll be honest with you – I can really tell, 'cos as you know, when you're driving, and driving on country lanes, the passenger seat is oblivious [*sic*] – you've just got your eyes on the road and that is it.

There passes a period of time measured by the newspaper accounts in terms of the approximate distance covered by the speeding van – one mile, perhaps two, which if Roy was doing 'forty minimum' would mean about three minutes. This, of course, is an estimate drawn from the witness's recollection of the events and it is not remarkable that during our conversation Roy was inclined to think the time-span was possibly longer: 'I suppose I was driving for – what, four, five or six minutes'. The fact remains that it was at this moment that Roy decided to make his friendly gesture, which allowed him to realize the hitcher was missing ('and when I turned round to offer him a cigarette, the bloke had gone') but not to appreciate exactly *when* the disappearance had taken place. Hence he could not be sure of how long the pale-faced young man had remained next to him in the car.

Roy's reaction to the discovery is instinctive: he applies the brakes (the *Dunstable Gazette* suggests that the car did not come to a full halt) and rapidly checks to ensure the man has not crawled unobserved into the rear of the van, though this he knows to be an impossible possibility. It is equally unrealistic to suppose the fellow had leapt (*also* unobserved and without activating the interior light!) from the van as it travelled at 'about forty minimum'. The road behind was empty; the flat farmlands offered no hiding places even if the man *could* have made a surreptitious exit from the car – although it is worth remembering that the incident was alleged to have taken place at night, when it was 'as black as it would have got'. Full comprehension dawning upon him, Roy suddenly felt very cold, yet his hands perspired. He drove off as fast as he could to his local.

'You look as if you'd seen a ghost,' commented someone as Roy came in.

'Yeah,' replied Roy grimly, 'I *have*'.

Aftermath

Despite a dislike for whisky, Roy was gripped by an overwhelming desire for a large Scotch. He then told his strange tale to the patrons of the bar and made his way to Dunstable Police Station – not so much in the hope of 'getting something done' about his adventure as to see whether there had been other reports of similar ghostly happenings.

Some weeks before meeting Roy I had telephoned the Dunstable Constabulary to ensure that the facts given in the *Sunday Express* article – and especially the attitude attributed to Inspector Rowland – were essentially correct. It seems they were. Roy Fulton – an 'ordinary sort of chap', Inspector Rowland recalled – had indeed reported a vanishing passenger, and though his story caused the elevation of a few eyebrows a car was sent to the scene of the incident. As might have been predicted by the least psychically-gifted of persons, the investigators found nothing and no one. Having done all that they felt could reasonably be achieved, the police withdrew. We can sympathize with their conclusion that this was not the sort of case upon which they could profitably expend much time.

From Roy Fulton's point of view, police response to his allegation was noncommittal: 'They never actually gave me a yes and a nay on it, they just took the statement and they never said, 'We'll be in touch', or anything like that. I just gave them what I'd seen and they said no more'. There was no suggestion that the witness should be taken out to Station Road for on-the-spot inquiries; I gather that the place is sufficiently well known for the police officers to have deduced where to go from his description.

I've been out there *since* then, but not on the night of the occasion. I never went back out there [that night] . . . I've been down there [since] but I must admit it wasn't dark at the time; it was still daylight. I mean, I drive through there on the way from Leighton Buzzard coming home. I still come that way, but I must admit . . . in daylight.

Roy was of the opinion that he is not the only person to have picked up the Hitch-Hiker. The Dunstable Police told me they knew of no comparable reports on this theme – a negative echoing Inspector Rowland's remarks on the rarity of such stories as quoted by the *Sunday Express*.[3] Anne Cox was kind enough to check the issues of the *Dunstable Gazette* for the weeks following publication of her 'Night Ride Riddle' piece in case they carried any correspondence from people who claimed to have undergone experiences similar to that of Roy Fulton. Nothing of the kind was to be found, and even a conjectured connection with a tragic accident failed to find support from firm evidence.

Anne had concluded her story with a short paragraph based (she told me) on information provided by the son of one of Mrs Fulton's friends. While working on a school project about local ghost stories, the boy had come upon a tale of a young Scotsman reputedly run over and killed while hitch-hiking home from a party; the implication was that this anonymous character could provide the key to the identity of Roy's taciturn passenger. With commendable industry Mrs Cox searched newspaper files for six years back, consulted the local police and some of the Stanbridge residents. Finding no evidence that such a fatality had occurred, she was forced to discount the truth of it and presented the digression as only a rumour or folk-story at the end of her article. The *Sunday Express* made no reference to this tragic-accident victim, and nor did Roy Fulton when I spoke to him.

A critic could argue that here, in this uncorroborated piece of folklore unearthed by a schoolboy's local history project, was the material upon which Roy Fulton drew for his ghostly narrative. This suggests that for reasons of his own the carpet-fitter decided to appropriate the Scots Hitch-Hiker yarn and retell a truncated version of it with himself as the hero; or perhaps the truncation was enforced by the fact that he knew few details concerning the ghost. A gentler approach would be to hypothesize that the act of memorization was neither deliberate nor conscious – that the tale impressed the hearer on a *sub*conscious level and later came to life in a most unexpected fashion: a curious form of revived memory expressed as a hallucination.

This joint-hypothesis is dependent upon a triple assumption. To memorize the story either consciously or subconsciously Roy Fulton would have had to have heard it from the boy, the boy's mother, from his own wife or from some other source, *before* 12 October – the night on which he claimed to have picked up the pallid-faced apparition. Unhappily, there is no evidence to show that he *had* or had *not* heard the story prior to this seminal date. Even if the former proposition were seen to be true, there is nothing to prove beyond all doubt that the tale impressed him enough to remain in his mind, and still less to indicate the way in which it lent form and modulation to his story (if fabricated) or experience (if hallucinatory). By its fundamental nature it is not a hypothesis amenable to testing.

Two kinds of bird

There is a simple choice of response to the Phantom Hitch-Hiker of Stanbridge. Roy Fulton *could* have invented a plausible-sounding implausible story. The most convincing aspects of it – the *sex* of the ghost, its *mute* condition, its *lack of purpose* (no proof of identity offered, no data indicating it was a surviving spirit) – are departures from the folklore norm of loquacious female Hitch-Hikers whose conversation inevitably leads to a tidy, satisfyingly rounded conclusion; but that may be either a tribute to the narrator's judgement as to what convinces researchers, or conversely a condemnation of his lack of imagination. Dunstable may contain persons who will enjoy this chapter immensely, knowing the apparition to be a grand fake, a hoax. It would not be the first time a fabricated ghost story, well known as such to those in the area in which it is set, has been made respectable in print. (And as someone once remarked, in Phantom Hitch-Hiker stories it is not the ghost that gets taken for a ride as much as the listener. Naturally, this could equally apply to parapsychologists.)

The alternative is to concede that Roy Fulton spoke in good faith – that notwithstanding the correspondences between his story and those all too familiar to folklorists as 'urban legends' or 'whale tumour stories' (fiction represented as fact), he was honestly describing what he believed had happened.

There is a saying that one swallow does not make a summer. Even if Roy Fulton's story sounds true, a sceptic could protest, this fails to alter the dubiousness of the Phantom Hitch-Hiker as a whole and it is more sensible to say that the mass of evidence proving the motif is fictive ought to make us reject one stray example where the evidence (perhaps by chance) could be interpreted in the other direction. But crows are as important as swallows – and there is an equally well-known proverb to the effect that the existence of one white crow proves that all crows are not black. In short, those who choose to believe the Stanbridge story will know that not all Phantom Hitch-Hiker tales are fiction. It comes down to personal attitude.

At any event, the brevity and conciseness of the Stanbridge episode has a lot to recommend it. The saga of Blue Bell Hill's allegedly-recurrent Phantom Hitch-Hiker provides a distinct contrast to this state of affairs.

SIX: THE HAUNTED HILL

The opening of the present dual carriageway stretch of the A229 – the most direct route for a motorist heading out of Maidstone towards Chatham – superseded a short, steep climb that emerged just north of the Lower Bell public house. Officially known today as the Old Chatham Road, this used to enjoy a more decorative name still attached to the community nearby: it was called Blue Bell Hill.

The Hill appears to have exerted an unfathomable influence over the human imagination for the better part of 4000 years. One of southern England's most famous Neolithic monuments – Kit's Coty House – stands in an adjacent field, with the considerably disturbed 'Countless Stones' (or Little Kit's Coty House) not far from it. The *Victoria County History of Kent* adds that scattered stones just above Kit's Coty House were thought by Mr Thomas Wright to be the coverings of sepulchral chambers, though excavations in 1844 revealed quantities of flints rather than bones.[1] In general terms such data suggests that around 4000 years ago the Blue Bell Hill area was associated with some kind of monumental preservation of either human remains or artefacts.

Blue Bell Hill can be characterized as one of those places that attracts to itself a canon of weird stories, just as a fallen tree will provide the focus for a growth of fungi. It is less surprising that the Hill has a ghost story than the ostensibly modern form the ghost takes. Anyone who delves into the local rumour-legends, their variations and contradictions, will probably identify *several* ghost stories yoked together by the same evasive but familiar Phantom Hitch-Hiker motif.

The unfolding story
Some writers have tried to establish a romantic connection between Blue Bell Hill's Neolithic residents and its Phantom Hitch-Hiker. At the time of Maurice Goodenough's strange

Adjacent to Blue Bell Hill, Kit's Coty House (above) and (below) Little Kit's Coty House (also known as the 'Countless Stones') have been loosely and conjecturally linked with the Phantom Hitch-Hiker. (*author's photograph*)

encounter with a small girl who vanished, for example, *The Gazette* (Maidstone) observed that the road up the Hill runs across the site of numerous prehistoric graves, some of them 'known' to be related to occult practices.[2] True though this may be, the history of Britain's most famous ghostly Hitch-Hiker seems unlinked to ancient sorceries or their modern counterparts. Nor has the Hill any marked reputation as an accident 'black spot', something which might arguably generate talk of curses, apparitions and ill-luck. Curiously, the A20 near Lenham *has* that kind of notoriety but no ghost – curiously, because amid the frightful death-toll it logged some two and a half decades ago occurred one incident tailor-made for a Phantom Hitch-Hiker story when on Saturday 10 August 1968 a hitch-hiker was accidentally struck and killed by a motorist.[3] Again, local journalists referring in 1974/75 to 'The Hill of Death' had in mind the road outside Detling to the northeast of Maidstone, where four fatalities and three serious injuries earned it an unenviable character. The paradox is that, to the best of my knowledge, neither is supposed to be haunted by a road-ghost – whereas Blue Bell Hill, with a much lower quota of crashed cars and lost lives, certainly has that repute. An evil traffic record is not in itself sufficient to merit a ghostly reputation, then, although it will be interesting to see whether rumours begin to settle about Lenham or Detling over the next few years.

Though I stand to be corrected, the first printed reference to the Blue Bell Hill haunt may have appeared in *The Gazette* (Mid-Kent's picture paper, one of the Kent Messenger group) of 10 September 1968.[4] Apart from putting down in black and white the essential, perhaps primary, version of the story, it highlighted the fact that Mr Tom Harber, a blind switchboard operator at Oakwood Hospital, Barming, had been trying to locate actual witnesses of the latterly famous phantom.

The reporter's opening sentence spoke of repeated appearances of the girl who waits at the foot of the Hill – 'Everything points to her being a ghost' – and thereby implied that the story had been circulating for some time beforehand. The version given here may have crystallized any number of rumours and perhaps helped to 'define' the tale as it was later told. The girl (unidentified, of course) behaves in a thoroughly traditional Hitch-Hiker manner. Having made contact at the bottom of the Hill near the Lower Bell public house, she chats to motorists all the way to the vicinity of Week Street (a busy shopping thoroughfare leading into the heart of Maidstone), where she vanishes. Only the critical folklore element in which the motorist confirms the girl's identity (and deceased status) by calling at a given address is absent from this article. After several months' searching, Mr Harber was said to have failed in his quest to find anyone who was prepared to say that this had actually happened to him or her. He had received eighty or ninety telephone calls about local ghosts and related matters, but all thirty of those concerning Blue Bell Hill's Hitch-Hiker were secondhand tales; Mr Harber could not even obtain a description of the apparition.

So far, as folklorists would surely accept, the story runs true to type: an utterly conventional Version A Phantom Hitch-Hiker account, the witnesses to which are (also as per convention) untraceable. What they and many others would *not* accept, however, was the assertion made to me by Mr Harber during three lengthy telephone conversations and an afternoon's face-to-face discussion: that eventually this researcher traced and interviewed no less than twelve persons who claimed to have encountered Blue Bell Hill's hitch-hiking ghost.

One eyewitness to the Phantom Hitch-Hiker strains credibility, perhaps; a round dozen threatens to abolish it completely. Since I have not met any of Tom Harber's informants it follows that I cannot vouch for them nor offer an independent assessment of their stories. We are left with the statements of Mr Harber himself that he carefully cross-examined each in person and separately; that he watched for contradictions during subsequent retellings of the accounts and went back to several of them after the initial interviews. And finally that he concluded their testimonies were 'all solid'.

From this process a number of points emerged, many of them convincing 'negatives'. The witnesses did *not* give perfect descriptions full of minute detail: 'if they had', Tom told me, 'I'd have known it was a load of nonsense', for witnesses rarely display total accuracy of recall on matters of dress and appearance. All assumed the girl to have been a real person – at least at the start of the experience: not transparent, not at all ghostly in form or manner. They presented varied yet plausible rationalizations to explain why none had felt it strange that a girl (who by her own admission was to be married next day) should be hitch-hiking alone at such a late hour and in such an isolated place. Tom Harber decided he had been talking to 'twelve down-to-earth persons, and not your maiden aunts, who'd believe anything.'

Indeed, one of them continues to believe to this day that he had a living girl with him in the car, though the evidence for this is rather unencouraging. The witness, known 'extremely well' to Mr Harber, who says he questioned the man less than twenty-four hours after the alleged incident, claimed the girl had talked about her wedding next day as they drove to Maidstone. Later the motorist visited the address she had given him to check on her safety. His concern for her well-being came too late; she had been killed in a car crash a year before on the very day he had met the Hitch-Hiker by the Lower Bell.

This 1966 incident was the first of Tom Harber's cases, the one that caused him to seek out more. In due course he interviewed others – an ambulanceman, a Post Office driver, and so on – who had undergone similar encounters with the Week Street girl; two cases featured more than one witness and could therefore be classed as collective sightings. 'I have never found such a well-tallied set of accounts,' he declared during our second conversation. The events they described were the same, as were the timings (that is, all occurred at 11 p.m.); the only divergent note was that in a few instances the girl wanted to go to Chatham rather than Maidstone.

Here is an anniversary ghost and tragic death motif to perfection. The trouble is that we are not asked to digest it as folklore, but as literal fact. This summary of Tom Harber's researches and conclusions is offered just as it was offered to me. By their nature they must remain articles of faith for those disposed to share Mr Harber's acceptance of them and as inadmissibly uncorroborative matter for those who are not. The fact remains that the twelve witnesses and the tales they told never appeared in print, whereas others did – with confusing results.

Published stories

Following the aforementioned article on Tom Harber's supposedly negative quest, the *Kent Evening Post* of 27 February 1969 dubbed the place 'Blue Bell Hill – the driver's nightmare!' when describing how Mr David Smith of Rochester was having doubts about two pedestrians. Normally they could be seen walking *up* the Hill on the pavement until he was within a few yards of them, whereupon they vanished. But on another occasion they were promenading *down* on the opposite, pavementless side when he observed the pair rush abruptly into the path of a vehicle, which drove straight through them leaving no trace of mangled remains nor any other physical clue to their presence in its wake.

These particular pedestrians likewise disappear forever from the material in my possession and may be regarded as no more than an unexpected reward for the anomaly collector. More typical of the Blue Bell Hill canon are the brief concluding paragraphs of this little article, containing another reference to the still-undescribed girl who wants to go to Week Street and is gone before she gets there. The digression, tacked somewhat freely onto Mr Smith's vanishing walkers, sounds like a rehash of the details given a year before in the *Maidstone Gazette's* piece on Tom Harber, with the difference that the girl is now reputed to await her lift at the top of the Hill instead of at the bottom.

Nothing more concerning the Hitch-Hiker was reported for some little time afterwards. But with the approach of the next Christmas, the proper season in Britain for the telling of weird tales, she was on the road again, as a sceptical journalist from one of the *Kent Messenger* papers noticed. During the first week of December two unsubstantiated motorists' stories of 'this now celebrated girl hitch-hiker' reached the writer, causing him or her to speculate that either the earth-shifting machinery and roadworks in the area had antagonized the ghost world or that the Yuletide appetite for eerie narratives was responsible for her renaissance. Both the status of the Blue Bell Hill phantom and the journalist's own response to her was summed up by a reference to 'that old chestnut of a ghost story' – an undeniably in-season metaphor.[5]

As if intimidated by the implied slight, the phantom attracted no further press attention until 1974. Apart from guitarist Richard Studholme's 'Blueberry Hill' adventure described in Chapter Four (which may date from this time), this was the year of Maurice Goodenough's variation on the basic Vanishing Hitch-Hiker theme: the witness did not pick up the girl but knocked her down, not long after which her body disappeared in what impressed reporters as a 'ghostly' fashion. For this reason the story was treated as part and parcel of the Blue Bell Hill series, despite its containing more than one departure from type. Mr Goodenough put the age of the small girl he'd struck at about ten years – an estimate seeming to conflict with the mature heroine featured in the 1968-70 articles. Had the writers of these previous pieces observed the apparent youth of the purported phantom we would have expected them to have commented upon, if not made capital from, the fact.

Having stimulated the most extensive police and press interest to date, the Phantom Hitch-Hiker faded from the limelight. This may not have been her finale; one resident on the Hill told me that only a few months after searching fruitlessly for the 'schoolgirl' Mr Goodenough's car had hit, the police received an almost identical collision story from another man. This time there was no press coverage and it seems that the authorities suspected one of those derivative or imitative hoaxes which members of the public sometimes perpetrate from a desire (one presumes) to attract attention. It is open to debate as to whether anyone would regard a recent ghost story as a promising model upon which to fantasize or fabricate; also it would demand a very ingenuous liar to try out so doubtful a yarn on the police, who do not take kindly to having their time wasted. Once again, though, this orally-collected testimony is scarcely amenable to corroboration; it must be taken at face value – or not at all.

If it resulted in little else, Mr Goodenough's accident-that-wasn't demonstrated how the Blue Bell Hill haunting was linked in the minds of some people with a car crash in 1965 (or 1967, depending on sources) which took the lives of three young women, one of whom was to have been married the following day. *This* is the sort of detail which *can* be verified, although it is another matter to associate such a proven fact with the ghost stories supposedly originating from it.

Accident report

Maidstone Divisional Headquarters of the Kent Constabulary is quite familiar with the Phantom Hitch-Hiker of Blue Bell Hill – that is, with the local tale concerning the ghost of a girl killed there on the eve of her wedding. Records of any such accident are a different thing. As I learned from the authorities, a policy of preserving this type of document for only five years means the paperwork would have been destroyed sometime in the 1970s.

Nonetheless, it is almost certain that the crash alluded to in the Blue Bell Hill ghost saga was one that occurred late in the evening of Friday 19 November 1965. The facts as given in the regional press at that time support the opinion, though (quite typically) they do not dovetail precisely with memories of the event invoked to 'explain' the Phantom Hitch-Hiker.

As reported by the *Maidstone Gazette*, a 22-year-old girl was fatally injured a matter of hours before her wedding at St Mary's Church, Gillingham, when the car (a Ford Cortina) carrying herself and three female companions from an eve-of-wedding party was in collision with another (a Jaguar) on Blue Bell Hill.[6] She died five days later in West Kent Hospital. A 23-year-old female passenger was killed outright and a third girl was seriously injured. The fourth victim, who died on admission to hospital, was to play an unusual role in subsequent Hitch-Hiker stories referring back to the incident as a possible explanation: in some almost para-logical fashion she was cast as the most

The crossroads at the foot of Blue Bell Hill, scene of a fatal car crash in November 1965 and subsequently believed to be one of the points where the Phantom Hitch-Hiker awaits a lift. (*author's photograph*)

likely human original of Blue Bell Hill's Phantom Hitch-Hiker. Although her name has been given in various accounts of the haunting, I prefer to designate her (after her home town) as 'the Rochester girl'. For sake of completeness, it can be added that the occupants of the other car both survived the crash.

According to the thesis explored up to this point, the Blue Bell Hill phantom may have been *either* relocated or regional variations on an old, received motif (folklore) *or* veritable apparitional encounters which, rightly or wrongly, became associated with the memorized fact of the 1965 accident. What is more certain is that many of these episodes derived a species of credibility or even respectability from the indisputably-real crash, which lent the ghost story a readily acceptable and logical explanation. We may agree that there is a certain emotional or artistic rightness about the line of thought that proposes that the spirit of a tragically-slain girl is trying to complete her cruelly-terminated last journey. It is easy to forget that the relationship between tragic death and hauntings, though widely believed in, is one only occasionally supported by the evidence of psychical research.

Hard logic is ill suited to cases of this type, as is shown in the variant behaviour of the Blue Bell Hill phantom(s). In some accounts heard by Dennis Chambers, another local researcher, the girl is silent and is assumed to be the spirit of the bride-to-be. In others, the passenger is talkative to the point of garrulousness on the subject of a forthcoming wedding and (for unclarified reasons) is identified as one of the *other* girls. The ghost is encountered at various points on the Hill; a young lady who lives there told me the Hitch-Hiker has also been picked up at the bus-stop near the top of the Hill *and* on the dual carriageway by Medway-bound drivers. This raises the conundrum as to why the ghost should sometimes wish to travel towards Chatham (or other Medway towns) and sometimes in the opposite direction (towards Maidstone). Joan Forman explains this ambiguity or vacillation by suggesting it indicates some measure of freewill in the Other World; the apparition, far from being a pattern-shackled creature doomed to repeat *ad nauseum* the same actions in the same places, can actually decide for herself whether to travel north *or* south.

The account of the Blue Bell Hill enigma in Ms Forman's *The Haunted South* introduces several interesting variations on details reported in the Kent press at the time of the crash.[7] Her correspondent states that it happened on a miserably inclement *Thursday* night in November 1965 as the girls drove towards a pub to meet the fiancé; the collision at the foot of the Hill is replaced by the car skidding off the road at a bend and (most remarkable of all) descriptions of the Hitch-Hiker are said to favour the belief that the Rochester girl – a bridesmaid, not a bride-to-be – was the original victim whose spirit now haunts the Old Chatham Road. I have been able to confirm that Ms Forman's source of information based what he gave her upon local newspaper accounts written some nine years after the accident; the trip to the pub after trying on wedding dresses, the car leaving the road at a treacherous bend and co-identification of the Rochester girl with the Phantom Hitch-Hiker appeared in at least two articles by Nigel Nelson that were contemporary with the Maurice Goodenough encounter.[8] Unfortunately I have been unable to contact this writer to establish where he gleaned these deviant facts. Turning to the articles themselves with the assurance that they constituted the sum of Ms Forman's correspondent's own knowledge, I was especially puzzled as to what made Mr Nelson decide the ghost was that of the Rochester bridesmaid. Tom Harber, when I asked him, was equally at a loss to explain it.

Nevertheless, the articles quoted Tom in some detail on the characteristics of the Blue Bell Hill haunting. He told the journalist that the incidents usually occurred after 11 p.m. and that the apparitional girl might be met by drivers heading in either direction, up or down the Hill. However, those bound north towards Chatham could expect to be flagged down by a rather reserved young lady who volunteered the information that she had been involved in a motor accident and asked to be taken to Rochester. Mention of this town by Mr Harber, or the fact that Maurice Goodenough also came from there, may have forged a connection in the writer's mind with the detail that one of the 1965 victims was a Rochester girl; by carrying *her* photograph alongside its original front page account of the tragedy (not that of the bride-to-be) the *Maidstone Gazette* may have unwittingly thrown out a 'clue' to the ghost's identity for later researchers. Suffice to say that when presented with the idea that his daughter was now haunting Blue Bell Hill, the deceased's elderly father was as mystified as everyone else.

Two ghosts, one ghost or no ghost at all? Even by the normally confused evidential standards of Phantom Hitch-Hiker stories the Blue Bell Hill case seems outstanding.

The Goodenough encounter

So far the story, as the press portrays it, is regrettably deficient in the names and personal details of witnesses that psychical researchers like to have set before them. Years ago, as we have seen, Mr Tom Harber managed to follow up some privately-obtained leads and satisfied himself that there had been genuine apparitional encounters; he also claims to have spoken to one unique, *named* witness whose experience – sufficiently impressive to merit police action – had been spread abroad by national as well as regional newspapers. Unluckily, this publicity had a detrimental effect; the witness, tired of being castigated as a drunkard or lunatic, took the only sensible course by refusing to talk about his adventures any further. But even by the time this decision had been forced upon him, Maurice Goodenough's dramatic close-quarters confrontation with the vanishing ten-year-old girl in July 1974 had become the best-known and best-evidenced of all the Blue Bell Hill episodes.

In many ways, though, it was atypical of them – atypical, because it did not partake of the classic hitch-hiking/disappearing mature female structure common to the other stories. If anything, it is more reminiscent of David Smith's intangible pedestrians of 1969. Passing over this analogue, let us turn to the press reports of the time and reconstruct (as closely as we

The curve of Blue Bell Hill. One researcher believes this marked the scene of the 1974 Maurice Goodenough encounter. (*author's photograph*)

can hope to do so) the event which befell Mr Goodenough, adding for clarity a few important subsidiary details gleaned from other sources.[9]

The encounter took place shortly after midnight on the morning of Saturday 13 July 1974. The girl appeared from nowhere in the car's headlights, as though she had sprung up out of the ground. Mr Goodenough braked hard, skidded and registered the impact as he hit her. Alighting from his vehicle, he found the victim lying on the road, her knees skinned and her forehead bleeding. She looked to be about ten years old; her hair was dark brown and shoulder-length and she wore a lacy white blouse, white ankle socks and skirt. One detail confined as far as I can see to *The News of the World's* description of the incident was the witness's assertion that the casualty had moved her head and muttered 'Mummy', two or three times.

Mr Goodenough carried her to the pavement running along the western side of the road and wrapped her in a blanket – or a tartan rug, says Nigel Nelson.[10] He tried unsuccessfully to wave down about four passing cars and then rushed off for help. Various Kent papers mention his statement that he did not put the girl into his car because he was unaware of what injuries she might have received; nor could he see a telephone box. He drove into Rochester Police Station and made his report; the police then took up the search to find only the blanket. The supposedly injured victim had disappeared and the Blue Bell Hill ghost saga was about to recommence.

The search covered both sides of the Hill, which in July must have been richly clothed in foliage. At dawn a tracker dog was brought in, the investigation now being hampered by heavy rain.[11] Literal-minded people might maintain that this alone accounted for the police finding no bloodstains and their dog no track to follow. Subsequent inquiries at hospitals in the area revealed no admitted cases to fit the description of the mystery-girl; another interesting negative was that no marks or dents were found on Mr Goodenough's car.

The journalists were doubtless delighted when a police spokesman described the incident as the latest in a series of strange occurrences reported since the deaths of two girls in a car crash eight years ago on that very spot (though oral informants lead me to believe the Goodenough encounter took place further up the Hill than the Cortina-Jaguar collision). The same speaker then summarized the essential Blue Bell Hill accounts, citing – but not naming – several motorists and one motorcyclist as witnesses; one had reputedly called at the Gillingham address given by the girl before she vanished, only to learn his passenger had died on the Hill several years before. Although one of the 1965 victims was staying at Gillingham at the time of the accident, this seems to be the first occasion that town intrudes in the Blue Bell Hill story. There is another more obvious problem in connecting Mr Goodenough's ghost-girl with the spirits of *any* of the 1965 trio: if apparitions manifest according to their physical appearance at the time of their demise, it is hard to see how any of the three girls, all of whom were in their early twenties, could pass for the small child of under half that age he claimed to have hit.

The trail peters out
The Goodenough encounter seems to stand apart from the mainstream Blue Bell Hill stories conjecturally linked with the 1965 crash, and in some ways it is a pity it has become so entangled in the general mythos of the area. Even taken in isolation, the blended accounts raise several questions, not least those relating to the witness's activities in the interim period between the 'accident' and the arrival of the police on the scene. Put succinctly, inquiries to various Kent constabularies produced contradictory evidence. One said that Mr Goodenough preceded his visit with a telephone call (an understandable action for someone just involved in what he assumed was a serious accident); another stated that no such warning call was received and that the first notification they had was the arrival of the motorist to file his report in person. It is incontrovertible, however, that at 12.15 a.m. Mr Goodenough appeared at Rochester Police Station. If nothing else, this action – and the police's response to it – strongly indicates that the witness was reporting what to him was an all-too-genuine incident.

Evidently he was thinking in terms of a human traffic casualty, and the police investigated in the same frame of mind: the 'supernatural' interpretations were to follow. In the rainy, early morning blackness they were all looking for a small human being who had been hit by a car, *not* for a Phantom Hitch-Hiker. The mode and character of the search – still remembered by one resident on the Hill, who was awakened by the police and asked if her daughters were indoors – points to the fact that there was no suggestion of paranormal occurrences – yet.

This line of thinking clearly worked from the premise that, left to herself as the anxious motorist drove off to find help, the little girl had crawled away into the night. Or even *walked* away, her bloody injuries being superficial, or at least less severe than Mr Goodenough conceived as he saw her lying before him. Ms

Forman tackles this theory when she asks why, if this were the case, the girl left no traces behind her and why no medical records relating to consequent medical treatment arose. Did the rain remove the first and the sustaining of minor cuts obviate the second? The police found no sign of the girl after what sounds like a prolonged search, but this is not evidence that she may not have found her way to some refuge long before they started operations. Given the leafy cover, the rain and the darkness, her movements across the area may have gone undetected.

Though there must inevitably be doubts – how fast was Mr Goodenough travelling at the time, for instance? – minor injuries do not seem entirely out of sympathy with his account of the girl's appearance right after the collision. Ignoring this, it seems inevitable that – injured or not – she would have been forced to make her way home sooner or later. Why, when all the newspaper fuss was going on, did no one come forward with an explanation?

Did someone have a motive for keeping quiet about a certain person's absence – and/or did that person herself wish to avoid any involvement with what was turning into a ghostly mystery? One intriguing idea mooted at the time was that the police guessed the girl was 'on the run' –perhaps from one of the local child care centres. Whether this suggestion is pertinent or not, it is interesting that only three months before this incident two unhappy eleven-year-old girls were intercepted by police on Blue Bell Hill after they had absconded from a Maidstone school. Recollections of this event may well have been revived during the July search.[12] Fear of being found at a late hour when (and where) she ought not to have been would have provided the elusive young lady with an excellent reason for a swift recovery and exit.

By heaping suppositions one on top of the other – the girl was supposedly human, supposedly less hurt than she appeared to be and supposedly motivated towards a rapid disappearance – it is possible to avoid the conclusion that the 'accident victim' was something other than human. At first sight, the lack of success registered by the police tracker dog may be interpreted as a point in favour of the incident's paranormality – in theory, a human girl would have left a scent for the animal to pick up; a ghost would not. A telephone call to Chief Inspector Clark of the Essex Police Dog School showed that however conclusive the 'clue' of the scentless blanket may appear to laypersons, it cannot be used to validate the theory that the little girl was scentless as well, and therefore apparitional.

Chief Inspector Clark points out that tracker dog work involves consideration of a great many factors. In ideal conditions, ground scent will deteriorate with time; it lasts longer if the impressed surface happens to be grass. Quite apart from the fact that a certain amount of time elapsed before the tracker dog team arrived on the Hill, they had the additional problem that the accident victim had been laid at the roadside, where a residue of exhaust fumes and burnt rubber from passing traffic would compete with the scent from her body, not to mention the conflicting trails laid down by human investigators at the scene.

We are led to suppose that even if the little girl's ground scent was unavailable or undetected, the blanket in which she was wrapped should have provided body scent. But the prevailing notion that the dogs are often or always set on the track by studying objects worn or dropped by their quarry is misleading. Even if the Goodenough blanket had contained some traces of 'usable' body scent, there is no guarantee that the police handler would have made it the focus of his search. Criminals, Chief Inspector Clark comments, do not make a practice of leaving convenient objects by which they may be traced, and for this reason it would be foolish to train dogs to work solely from such deposited clues. At the scene of an incident like the one discussed here, the handler would have been seeking any form of trail, not only one connected with the blanket. In the final analysis, the failure of the tracker dog neither confirms nor negates girl *or* ghost.

Interpreting the evidence

Something very curious seems to have happened on Blue Bell Hill in the early hours of Saturday 13 July 1974 –something that made a 35-year-old bricklayer drive post-haste to his local police station and file a report that involved the police in hours of investigation, something which left him shaken for several days afterwards. Soon Maurice Goodenough knew he had become part of a famous Kentish ghost story: a form of celebrity he did not really want.

Accepting that the experience was genuine, how can we explain what Mr Goodenough saw that night? Did he see a *ghost*?

That word carries a variety of meanings, paramount among which is one defining the phenomenon as the spirit of a deceased person. It is part of the convention that the ghost returns to haunt the scene of its death in a quasi-physical form, approximating to the one it possessed at the moment of 'passing over'; moreover, it is intent on completing a purpose left unfulfilled at the time of that terminal event. This is the sort of ghost popularly supposed to be behind the Phantom Hitch-Hiker of Blue Bell Hill.

As a confirmed believer in spirit survival (though certainly not a blinkered one), Tom Harber is convinced that all the Blue Bell Hill incidents he has heard of, including that featuring Maurice Goodenough, represent evidence of the bride-to-be who died after the 1965 car collision. He bases this principally on the descriptions of the Hitch-Hiker – which he states vary only circumstantially.

In his view, the young lady was undergoing more than usual excitement with her wedding so close at hand; this degree of emotional arousal, plus the trauma of the crash itself, were the impetus that made possible her continued existence in the physical world. 'She desperately did not want to die,' he declares. When invited to reconcile the contradictory or diametrically-opposed directions in which the Hitch-Hiker wants to travel (south to Maidstone at times, north to Chatham or Rochester at others), Tom theorizes that the former represents a trip home (since he believes she came from that town), while the girl sometimes waits for a ride in the opposite direction because this was the way her car was travelling on the night she died. To reiterate, he thinks that *all* the incidents can be attributed to the ghostly activities of the bride-to-be alone, not to those of any of her companions.

We can refuse to be flustered by the fact that the ghost-girl is not haunting the literal scene of her death (West Kent Hospital) but the place where the accident occurred that was ultimately responsible for it; Spiritualists would say that the apparition is fixated by the last earthly spot of which the girl had full awareness, not by the incidental detail of where she eventually passed on. But what of that vast age discrepancy which threatens to divorce Maurice Goodenough's experience from the rest of the Blue Bell Hill collection? Quite simply, Mr Harber does not feel that there really *is* a discrepancy.

The bride-to-be was in her twenties; Mr Goodenough thought the small girl he knocked down was only about ten years old, which seems to present insurmountable difficulties as far as the proposed 1965 crash-nexus is concerned. But Tom cautioned me to recall that this was an estimate reached by a driver confused by both nocturnal conditions *and* the sudden shock of being involved in what he could only presume to be a serious road accident. These nocturnal conditions may have been far from straightforward: one newspaper account states that heavy rain greeted the start of the police on-site investigation, which means that it may also have been raining (or drizzling) before that time. Coupled with the horror of an abrupt collision, the conditions of the post-midnight encounter on an unlit road were not ideal for a steady identification of the victim.

The witness based his age estimate of the girl on her size and dress, with special emphasis perhaps on her white ankle socks. Taken together, these details suggested that the victim was only about ten years old. Tom makes the ingenious point that people tend to make errors purely from placing too much stress upon, or faith in, externals like the influential nature of dress. The bride-to-be had been a small person, he says, and on the fatal night she had been 'dressed youngish' – like a schoolgirl, one might almost say. And she was wearing white ankle-socks.

Being unable to speak to the Blue Bell Hill witnesses or to those closely concerned in the fatal accident that occurred back in 1965, I can produce no independent corroboration of the girl's physique or what she was wearing at the time of the crash. Some readers may recall that around this time ankle socks were fashionable items of dress among teenagers and there is nothing ridiculous in the notion of girls 'dressing down' in a way that made it hard for a casual observer to assess their true ages. Mr Harber adds that more than one of his dozen first-person witnesses had been deluded by the apparent youth of the Hitch-Hiker.

Tom Harber has probably expended more time and effort on the Blue Bell Hill haunting than anyone else. Even if we cannot share his highly-developed Spiritualist interpretation of events purported to have transpired there, these labours command respect. But it is not disrespectful to say that there are several features within the published accounts that make it hard automatically to equate the phenomena with the 1965 crash, and hence with spirit survival.

—In the earliest of the stories (1966) the girl wants to go to Maidstone, gives an address there and vanishes by the time the car reaches Week Street. Thus Maidstone plays an important part in the canon as the 'home' the girl wants to reach; yet at the time of the accident the press stated that the bride-to-be had been staying in *Chatham*. Unless she was not residing with her parents on the eve of her wedding, the paradox is curious. Why should a homeward bound spirit be going to Maidstone if it *was not* her home?

—This 1966 sighting and others garnered by Tom Harber stressed the calendrical consistency of the Hitch-Hiker; the spirit of the bride-to-be celebrates the anniversary of her death by trying to negotiate her last, fatal journey of 19 November 1965. Unfortunately, not all the Blue Bell Hill incidents show this meticulous regard for the calender; specifically, the Goodenough affair took place on 13 July, *not* on 19 November.

—Even admitting the poorly-lit, nerve-wracking conditions under which Maurice Goodenough examined the girl he had run into, is it conceivable that he would have mistaken her real age at such close quarters? Can we follow the suggestion that his confusion would account for his failure to do so?

These are not cast-iron objections to Tom Harber's interpretation. Blue Bell Hill may offer better evidence for the Spiritualist approach to the Phantom Hitch-Hiker than most comparable story-cycles, where the exegis is really little better than an assumption or a guess. For those who accept this approach, then, Blue Bell Hill may appear a perfect specimen of the revelation of how Man survives the act of death; for folklorists, who will regard Tom Harber's dozen witnesses as 'friends of friends', it is a perfect specimen of Beardsley and Hankey's Version A Vanishing Hitch-Hiker. Many others may care to take a position somewhere between, conceding that at least one tragic accident is known to have transpired on the Hill and at least one officially-reported unusual occurrence, yet politely declining to say how the two events were connected, if at all.

The mysterious female apparition, uncrowned queen of British Phantom Hitch-Hikers, has of late been keeping very much to herself. The only recent newspaper reference I have seen to her treated the ghost as one of three stories pressmen hear too frequently – stories told as gospel truth, but which upon investigation always prove to be fictitious.[13] It seems that whatever her credentials may have been a decade or so ago, the Blue Bell Hill Hitch-Hiker is slipping back into the realms of folk-tradition once more.

SEVEN: INTERPRETATIONS AND IMPLICATIONS

In terms of purpose and behaviour, the Phantom Hitch-Hiker of folklore is a thoroughly conventional ghost: one who matches popular expectations of what a ghost is, what it does and why. She is the spirit of a deceased person, the victim of a tragic accident which prematurely terminated her earthly life, and she has a *purpose*. On a personal level her main motivation, especially on anniversaries of that sorry event, is to complete her unfinished homeward journey. Her intelligence may not extend to the realization she is dead (another convention), but it sustains co-ordinated thought and speech, which infallibly leads the witness to an address where he corroborates the fact his passenger could only have been a spirit. This in turn teaches us that death is not the concluding chapter of the human story.

Parapsychologists (who will want to substitute 'apparition' for 'ghost') are hard put to sustain this romantic image. It is not so much the case that parapsychology's collected, verified and factual accounts of apparitions flatly contradict the popular conception in which ghosts are the spirits of the dead who perform from more or less logical motives, usually connected with the circumstances of their passing over. But the central figures in those narratives tend to fall far short of their folklore counterparts. A survey of authenticated cases reveals that there *have* been instances of ghosts with a purpose, but that there have occurred many, many more where such purpose is missing, or not self-evident; there *have* been instances of talking apparitions, but none matching the awareness and linguistic ability of the typical Hitch-Hiker. Worse, the hallowed relationship between tragedies and hauntings is, on the same showing, feeble. And finally, several prominent researchers have gone even further, suggesting that apparitions, whatever else they are, may be *nothing whatsoever* to do with departed spirits.

Love, death and romanticism

By its adherence to the spurious folkbelief norms – norms based on an antique popular approach to apparitions, not upon substantiated evidence – the typical Phantom Hitch-Hiker account is suspect. Parapsychology's menagerie of mute, non-comprehending and unexplained spectres cannot help validate such a purposeful, loquacious ghost; the inference follows that, unlike them, it is not authentic but a creation of folklore artifice. The few accounts that carry some degree of conviction – Nunney, Stanbridge, Maurice Goodenough's 1974 encounter on Blue Bell Hill, perhaps the A38 Man in a Mackintosh and the Montpellier traveller – do so by *not* conforming to the established folk canon.

In essence these are stories that lack satisfactory endings: the behaviour of the presumed ghost hints at no discernible purpose and appears related to no known tragedy in the area concerned. Incomprehensible, open-ended or inconclusive tales, in which things just 'happen' without clues as to why, are not usual in the folk tradition, but they are a staple item in psychical research, whose vast literature is replete with ghosts that do little more than appear and then vanish forever. Equally persuasive, the credibility of these accounts derives from the existence of named witnesses. There seems irrefutable evidence that non-intoxicated if shaken drivers – 'people . . . in a state of virtual hysteria', to quote the Nunney police officer – have made what pose as *bona fide* reports of vanishing passengers direct to their local constabularies. The predictably unproductive nature of the ensuing police inquiries matters much less than the fact that those authorities were sufficiently moved to initiate any in the first place.

When investigators check a story that relies on a tragedy for its 'meaning' or validity they are more likely to find the oral testimony relating to that all-explaining event at fault than otherwise. Selecting one Phantom Hitch-Hiker seemingly compatible with background research, Beardsley and Hankey scanned the Berkeley city records in the hope of retrieving details of 'some factual occurrence, perhaps a peculiar or spectacular accident' which might relate to the heroine of the story, a professor's daughter killed (so the tale dictated) on the corner of Bancroft Way and College Avenue. The relative wealth of narrative data made the quest appear initially promising, yet they found no record of a serious accident at that locality for five years either side of the date mentioned in the story.[1] Perhaps this seminal date was misleading – perhaps the accident had taken place earlier than the researchers had been led to suppose, or even in another place which somehow became confused with Bancroft-College. But that is not the impression that emerges; one is more inclined to accept that Beardsley and Hankey's investigations were exhaustive. And as their sample covered sixty named localities, it is also tempting to concur with their judgement that 'Tracing the factual sources of all these stories would entail a great deal of effort and would probably yield completely negative results.'[2]

The implication may be that where this crucial evidence is lacking, the entire story is as bogus as the 'tragic accident' portion from which it draws its narrative consistency. But occasionally one may wonder whether a germ of fact has fallen prey to the natural habit of trying to round off an inconclusive incident by providing a cause to marry up with the effect – using a conjectured or rumoured 'tragic accidental death' as a legitimate escape route. Earlier we saw something along these lines arising from press descriptions of the Goodenough episode; it also entered into speculations on the Stanbridge case and took the form of a deceased American serviceman at Nunney. It is an example of how we project our own forms of logic onto events which by their character threaten to be illogical.

Still, the romanticism of violent accidental death seems to fulfil some deep-rooted need in us when it comes to ghost stories. Its dominance is statistically borne out in the 79 Beardsley and Hankey tales to which so much reference has been made; of the 28 deaths they came across in their study, 13 involved car crashes, and in 10 of these the girl was said to have died on the spot where the motorist hero-witness stopped to pick her up. The writers suspect that this element may have been inherited from other types of ghost story, a conclusion which seems highly plausible.

The tragic death of a young girl can be made doubly poignant if it can be seen to have come about as a result, however indirect, of love: another sound principle of traditional ghostly-yarn production, since in addition to the violence of the actual death the existence of heightened emotions is widely assumed to release the correct 'charge' to cause a haunting. 'She desperately did not want to die,' Tom Harber remarked of the 1965 crash victim said to be remembered in the Blue Bell Hill incidents discussed in the last chapter. This could be the epitaph of numerous hitch-hiking female phantoms – including Resurrection Mary of Chicago who walked out on her boyfriend after a row in the 1930s, was knocked down while hitching a lift and has never had a chance to make her peace with him.[3] If the girl died in an accident with her lover at the wheel – or at the handlebars, as in the case of the girl killed while riding pillion through the Mersey Tunnel, of which she was or is Hitch-Hiker in residence[4] – then the artistic criteria are respected; but it is equally effective to have her wasted in the act of hurrying to his side. We have seen that one version of the Blue Bell Hill accident depicts a bride-to-be and her maids mortally injured as they drive to meet the fiancé. We have also seen that the time factor makes this literally dubious, unless they were making for a public house which kept somewhat irregular opening hours.

The interrupted-tryst motif is developed with a vengeance in the recent Peshawar case cited briefly at the start of this book.[5] Police files were said to contain additional reports of the pretty girl in white who thumbed a lift from motorcycle patrolman Mahmood Ali on a mountain road and who, of course, vanished from the rear seat before he reached her required destination, the difference being that the three previous witnesses were alleged to have been killed while in quest of their disappearing companion, all in collisions with trucks. Acting on the suspicions of local villagers, Ali confirmed that the Hitch-Hiker was (or rather, had been) a twenty-year-old named Nassera Begum; a photograph of the dead girl on the wall of her home put the question of her identity beyond dispute. Nassera had been hit by a truck when walking along the road in search of her lover and it was supposed she was continuing to do so, luring unfortunate men to their deaths as a sort of revenge.

Folklorists will notice the Version C characteristic (the phantom as a vampiristic threat to the living), and also the identification-by-dead-girl's-picture submotif.

There is a melodramatic quality about the Peshawar case that makes it sound too good to be true. The stories found in parapsychology are backed by evidence – are authenticated – but their fragmentary nature leaves them, from an artistic point of view, too true to be good. Yet the findings of parapsychology are at best tentative, little more than hesitant conclusions drawn from analysis of a gamut of carefully-sifted accounts; it is inadvisable to use them as the final arbiter of incidents where the apparition flouts researchers' criteria to behave in an utterly folk-ghost manner. The following story from South Africa features a Phantom Hitch-Hiker who, on some evidence, is the spirit of a road accident fatality.

The Uniondale case

The juxtapositioning of motorcycling and love thwarted by violent death reappears in the local tradition which asserts that a

Hitch-Hiker regularly haunts the Barandas turn-off outside the town of Uniondale (SA). She is supposedly celebrating each anniversary of her demise in a road accident on 12 April 1968, waiting on cold wet nights for some kind of transport (preferably driven by an unaccompanied male) that will enable her to complete the journey she never finished. If printed material is to be trusted, she has found suitable companions on at least four occasions.

The most recent of these may have been twenty-year-old Andre Coetzee on Good Friday 1980, but his experience is also the least impressive – he merely felt a 'presence' behind him on his motorcycle that was later taken to signify that of the ghostly woman. It could more rationally be put down to prior awareness of the area's 'haunted' reputation, to self-suggestion or plain nervousness, if not to less creditable explanations like deliberate fabrication. Mr and Mrs Leonard Fraser's encounter with a white-robed, perhaps transparent figure near the turn-off seven years earlier could conceivably be criticized on similar grounds.[6]

The story really begins to grip the imagination with the strange ride of Dawie van Jaarsveld in 1978. The main problem in relating this and the equally unusual experience of Anton La (or Le) Grange is that the two main sources (David Barritt and Cynthia Hind) tell neither in quite the same way.[7] Clumsy as it may appear, the only accurate way of pointing out divergences between the accounts is to introduce a system of attribution notes with the authority for each individual variant cited within parentheses.

A light drizzle hugged the Barandas-Willowmore Road outside Uniondale at around 9.35 p.m. on 31 March 1978 (April 1978: *Hind*). Dawie van Jaarsveld, a corporal in the South African Army, was on the last leg of a 115-mile ride to see his girlfriend in Louterwater, his boredom kept at bay by the music of a transistor radio; this device (or more precisely, the earplug at one end of its lead) plays a relatively minor part in one version of the story but a decidedly major one in the other. The sight of an attractive brunette in dark trousers and top (blue top: *Hind*) on a lonely road under these rainy conditions gave him doubts, and though he halted to offer her a lift, Corporal van Jaarsveld kept his wits about him, the engine running and the bike in gear. He half-feared she might be a decoy for a gang of thugs who preyed on motorists lured into stopping for her.

The rider watched the girl carefully through his rear-view mirror as she walked up to where he was parked (*Barritt*). Turning his head, he asked if she wanted a lift but the noise of

Corporal Dawie van Jaarsveld, hero of the 1978 episode in the Uniondale Phantom Hitch-Hiker series. (*photograph courtesy of FATE Magazine*)

the engine and the music in his ear (not to mention the earplug itself) meant that he missed all but one syllable of what seems to have been an address she wanted to reach: ('-straat': *Barritt*). Explaining that he couldn't hear – and assuming the girl aimed at some part of Uniondale (*Hind*) – Corporal van Jaarsveld told her to nod if she wanted a lift, which she did.

Thereupon the corporal handed her his spare crash helmet and at the same time advised her to make use of a second radio earplug, because the music would keep her awake (*Hind*). Alternatively, Dawie unclipped the spare helmet and placed it on the girl's head (*Barritt*) while the young lady stared at him with no change of expression, as if he was transparent – a non-response that made the man's blood run at less than its normal temperature.

The machine had covered a few kilometres (*Barritt*) or about ten miles (*Hind*) when Corporal van Jaarsveld felt an odd bumping sensation and his bike slithered slightly. Fearing a flat tyre (*Hind*) he glanced back to find himself minus his pillion passenger. Had she fallen off? The motorcyclist retraced his journey, slewing his machine from side to side in the attempt to penetrate the darkness at the roadside with his headlight. A couple of kilometres more and the strange bumping returned; it was the spare helmet he'd lent to the girl, now loosely clipped to the luggage rack. In the Hind account, the helmet had been *securely* strapped to the *rear seat* and the girl was missing; not missing, though, was the spare radio plug – this Corporal van Jaarsveld located *in his own ear*, which defies the allegation that he hadn't taken off his own helmet since the ride began. These features suggest that the offer of the spare items and the girl's acceptance of them were truly paranormal incidents and it is a pity they do not figure at all in David Barritt's narrative.

There is likewise some disparity as to the conclusion of the van Jaarsveld story. Cynthia Hind confirmed by personal investigation that the witness had (as he had claimed) gone directly to the Petros café, Uniondale, into which he walked like the proverbial man who has just seen a ghost. The proprietress recalled the distracted condition of the visitor and affirmed that she believed he had met the local Phantom Hitch-Hiker. Next port of call for the researcher was the Louterwater farm, where one of the residents testified that Corporal van Jaarsveld had arrived in a state of some disquietude and that he told the family the tale next morning. David Barritt adds that the witness had positively identified his supernatural passenger from a photograph of a deceased road accident victim; unfortunately, he does not say how long after the event this identification was made.

The photograph showed Maria Charlotte Roux, a 22-year-old brunette who was killed at around 4.30 a.m. on 12 April 1968 when the car driven by her fiancé left the road through the Karoo Desert not far from Uniondale. These facts, together with the belief that the girl was the original of the Phantom Hitch-Hiker who haunts the road each Easter, seem to have emerged following publicity surrounding a 1976 encounter described in both Hind and Barritt articles. Once again, however, these writers are not in total agreement as to what happened.

Anton Le Grange (La Grange: *Barritt*) of Oudtshoorn encountered the Hitch-Hiker some 13 kilometres outside Uniondale at 7.15 p.m. on 1 May 1976 (12 May 1976: *Hind*). The combination of rain, cold and darkness encouraged the driver to offer a lift to a girl who was not, technically speaking, hitching; she was dark-haired and pale-faced (as in van Jaarsveld's account) and wore dark slacks plus a navy blue jacket with toggles (*Hind*: cf. a dark duffle coat in *Barritt*). She wanted a lift to 'De Lange, 2 Porter Street' (Porter Street 2, De Lange: *Barritt*). Mr Le Grange had only just put the car in motion when he recalled he was heading for Oudtshoorn and that there was no such street in that town. On turning to query the address he found the girl had vanished.

Now the order of events becomes somewhat confusing. Mr Le Grange certainly reported the incident to the Uniondale Police; Constable Potgieter, the duty officer, remembered his visit very well. It is what happened next that is problematical.

Constable Potgieter told Cynthia Hind that Mr Le Grange had come in, wild-eyed and desperate yet sober, and that his mood seemed urgent enough for the policeman to agree to accompany him to the haunted spot. On the way a very odd thing occurred: P.C. Potgieter saw the rear door of Mr Le Grange's new Mercedes open and shut as though someone (or something) had just got out – an event that may be explicable in terms of a faulty lock-hinge mechanism, or that may not be. As this happened, added Mr Le Grange, he heard a spine-chilling laugh.

In the Barritt version Constable Potgieter – although impressed by the sincerity of the motorist – first responded with the advice that he should forget about the incident. Mr Le Grange was endeavouring to do so when, driving away from Uniondale, a horribly hysterical scream from somewhere inside his car had him back-tracking to the police station in sheer terror. This time he would not be pacified and Constable Potgieter had to agree to follow behind in his van. From his elevated position he was well situated to observe the right rear door of the La Grange vehicle swing gently open as if controlled by someone in the act of alighting – though both cars were travelling at speed. So everyone admits that the door-opening incident *did* occur, but there is argument as to whether the fearful scream was heard before or after this episode. Mr Le

The Karoo desert road outside Uniondale, SA. This spot may be close to the scene of the accident in which Maria Roux – a candidate for the identity of the Phantom Hitch-Hiker – was killed. (*photograph courtesy of FATE Magazine*)

Grange was inclined to believe it was the death-cry of the girl, whom he later found had been the 1968 accident-victim (*Barritt*). For himself, Constable Potgieter was greatly impressed by the phenomenon of the opening door; both articles quote him as holding the belief that something paranormal had befallen the witness and (*Barritt*) that a ghost had been in the car. But *whose* ghost?

The obvious answer, encouraged by the Barritt statement that Mr Le Grange had decisively identified his passenger from a photograph, is that the spirit belonged to the unlucky young victim of a road accident in this desolate part of the country. Cynthia Hind, though, leaves us feeling a trifle less certain. She writes that after the Le Grange adventure had reached the papers, a Lieutenant Giel Pretorius of the SA Air Force asserted that the haunting related to the death of his fiancée (Maria Roux) who was killed on 12 April 1968 when a powerful wind threw their small car from the road and over an embankment. Lt. Pretorius produced a photograph of his fiancée, which elicited an immediate response from Mr Le Grange.

Contrary to the remarks attributed to him in the Barritt version, Mr Le Grange was not absolutely certain that the photograph showed the girl he had picked up – although he found the resemblance a very close one. There is additional information from the police sergeant who attended the 1968 crash that the deceased had been wearing dark green slacks and a navy blue duffle coat. All of which strengthens the impression that the two women were, incredibly enough, one and the same.

It was left to Ms Hind to tie up the loose ends of the story. The Porter Street address remains a mystery; Cape Town Publicity Bureau knew a street of that name only in Worcester, and No. 2 proved to be a boys' school hostel with no knowledge of 'De Lange'. The researcher was unable to reach Lt. Pretorius or Maria Roux's mother, who had moved elsewhere. We are left with the localized (Uniondale) legend that the spirit of the girl appears only on dark, wet nights around the Good Friday anniversary of her demise – and only when a solitary male driver comes along. Remarking that she knows of just two documented instances to support that premise, Cynthia Hind cites the opinions of various authorities. Dr Laubscher, a Port Elizabeth writer on the supernatural, thinks the thwarted love of Maria Roux has made her earthbound and accessible to persons with suitable psychic faculties; others speak more severely of 'subjective occurrences'. And with a few atmospheric comments on her own sojourn to the haunted spot, Ms Hind's fascinating article closes.

Looking with some difficulty past the assorted discrepancies in these accounts – applauding also that someone went to the trouble of trying to check the story by interviewing available witnesses – the Uniondale case may furnish the best evidence yet for the traditional interpretation of the Phantom Hitch-Hiker as a discarnate spirit. Of course, it depends as usual on the credibility of largely unsupported eye-witnesses, but there are two of them, *two* reporters and *two* separate incidents pointing in the direction of a ghost that obeys the folklore tenets concerning tragic origins and regularized (anniversary) appearances.

But reverting to Beardsley, Hankey *et al* it is clear that not all Hitch-Hikers are reputed to be ghosts of the tragically-slain; the Version B 'prophetics', for instance, seem to pertain to some other category of supernormal being. If behaviour is taken as a key to the Hitch-Hiker, these vanishing prophets whose predictions do not come true force us to look elsewhere for their origins. Deep into the realms of folklore once again.

Nightshapes

From a purely behavioural viewpoint, the Phantom Hitch-Hiker occasionally appears less like the spirit of a departed human and much more like one of the protean, mischief-bound entities whose fondness for lonely, benighted roads made nocturnal travel terrible for our distant forefathers. The sole delight of these bogies was to cause amazement and panic – the only motives assignable to the road-ghosts of Nunney and the A38, one might retort when attempting to apply logic to the eyewitness accounts. 'These walking spirits sometimes stop the way before men as they travel,' cautioned Lavater, 'and lead them out of their way and put them in . . . great fear . . .'.[8] In the same chapter he notes that among those most prone to suffer from these apparitions were 'carters' – perhaps the closest thing to our own modern motorists.[9]

In his paper on historical prototypes of the twentieth century Phantom Hitch-Hiker stories Professor Jones remarks on the tradition of supernatural, generally malevolent passengers who inveigle rides in horsedrawn vehicles. One example he cites is vaguely demonic; the other, distinctly witchlike, ends the tale by flying out of the buggy.[10] By very close analogy, in Malaysia the Phantom Hitch-Hiker is approximated in the *langsuyar*, a sort of vampire whose female charms seduce young men into offering her a lift whenever she lurks by the roadside. At a strategic spot – frequently in dense jungle or near a graveyard – the *langsuyar* persuades the driver to stop and promptly soars off into the night uttering blood-curdling screams. Harkening back to Mr Davidson-Acres' reported experience, we may conclude that a woman who merely and soundlessly vanishes is the lesser of the two Malaysian evils.[11]

With all classes of sprites, witches and ghosts assuming a Hitch-Hiker identity, it is not remarkable that Satan himself should be cast in the same role. Such is the implication if a ballad entitled 'The Devil and the Coachman, or, Man's Amazement', first printed around 1684, is to be taken literally. Perhaps readers *were* encouraged to believe that the anonymous composer was presenting an accurate summary of an authentic encounter, because he boldly invited any sceptics to visit the much-afflicted witness and look into the story for themselves:

> . . . in *Baldwin's Gardens* there in Cradle Court,
> This man still is living, as hundreds report,
> And those that will take but the pains for to go
> A further Account of the truth you may know;
> Yea, from his own mouth he will freely unfold
> The sum and the substance of what I have told.

According to the writer's full account, this strange-but-true adventure began after the coachman dropped a passenger in Water Lane. In the best Hitch-Hiker tradition, the Devil avails himself of the most popular form of contemporary transport, the tale thus relating to subsequent narratives in which the vehicle is a taxi-cab. He also observes the powerful convention of making himself as credibly human as necessary for the purposes of the deception:

> The Devil appear'd in the shape of a man,
> And leaning against a great post he did stand,
> With likeness of Parchment roll'd up in his hand.
> He call'd to the Coachman as it did appear,
> The Coachman supposing he had been a Fare . . .

This 'just Relation' ends, not with the Devil vanishing immediately but transformed into a bear which the coachman gallantly fends off with his whip. He escapes at the cost of limb paralysis, and 'Tis feared that he ne'er will recover again'. The ballad reminds us that not every age and culture has associated these transport-minded entities with the tragic spirits of the human dead. It is more true to say that they have been consistently interpreted according to prevalent cultural beliefs or subconscious needs.[12]

Hallucinatory Hitch-Hikers
While popular culture endows apparitions with a quasi-physical

life of their own, the science of parapsychology generally prefers to approach them as mental constructs, things of the mind. In this context the word 'hallucination' is commonly and unhappily employed – unhappily, because most of us continue to labour under the misconception that it is a perjorative label for an experience confined to the mentally disturbed, the drunk, the drugged. To tell a ghost-seer that he or she hallucinated the apparition is most often regarded as an insult – tantamount to suggesting that person is definitely abnormal, if not downright insane – and as an implication that the apparition itself was something that did not really 'happen'.

For over a hundred years now parapsychologists have been trying to explain that not only is there evidence that ordinary, well-balanced and sober people occasionally hallucinate, but that the unreality of these mental episodes is only relative. For the experient the hallucination *is* real, very real and it fulfils his/her everyday criteria as to what does or does not constitute reality; the fact that the hallucinatory figure has no solidly-physical existence is irrelevant.

The ghost-as-hallucination is only a suggestion of a particular (mental) mechanism which makes such things possible, a mind-state where a different level of reality applies. The hypothesis does not usually explain the source of the hallucination – why it took that particular form rather than some other – nor why it occurred at *that* time to *that* person. Extending the idea a little further, it is even feasible that spirits of the dead communicate (telepathically?) with the ghost-seeing witnesses, the resulting 'projection' being experienced by the latter on a mental level – as a hallucination.

On theoretical grounds alone the handful of Hitch-Hikers just segregated from their folklore counterparts obey standards laid down by G. N. M. Tyrrell of the Society for Psychical Research when he created a pen-portrait of the Perfect (hallucinatory) Apparition.[13] The phantom must always conform to the percipient's reality-gauge: what he/she accepts under normal conditions to be a product of reality. It must appear solid and three dimensional; it must react as we ourselves do to physical objects or obstructions. Roy Fulton's pale-faced young man gave no impression of being neither more or less than a human seeking a lift; he entered the van by opening its door rather than passing straight through it or materializing in the vacant seat. Tyrrell would argue that the apparition's ability to cope with a car door-handle – and the fact that this caused the interior lighting to come on – were only logical continuations sustaining the reality of the same illusion. Mr Fulton thought

Hallucinations are very real to those who experience them. Under the influence of stage hypnotist Ralph Slater two girls respond dramatically to the sight of imaginary mice. (*photograph courtesy of Gerald Duckworth and Co. Ltd.*)

he was seeing a normal person. A normal person could only get into a car via the door, which in turn would only be possible by manipulating the door-handle in the usual way; the witness also knew that this would have a natural result of activating the lighting circuitry. While, objectively speaking, the door did *not* open nor the light blink on, they *appeared* to the witness to do so because, in a sense, he expected those effects; they were additional constructs necessary to enhance the impression of reality/normality relating to the rest of the hallucinatory episode.

However cogent the proposed Hitch-Hiker hallucination, however *real*, there comes a point at which it can continue no longer. This is the natural quality of all hallucinations: they pass away. It is an illogicality and impossibility for them to endure permanently with the hallucinator captured in a sort of dream environment.

The precise reasons and psychological mechanics of this reversion to *status quo* are mysterious; if we continue to regard some Phantom Hitch-Hiker cases as hallucinatory we must realize that the 'snap-back' effect may be a very rapid one. The figure does not dwindle or fade into nothingness like Alice's Cheshire Cat – it is gone in an instant. However, this must remain a supposition because it is integral to the story that the witness does not catch the ghost in the vanishing act. He has not the leisure to monitor the actions of the person beside him; as Roy Fulton pointed out, the driver has the road to occupy his attention. But by implication the disappearance is sudden: one moment there are indications of someone in the passenger's seat, and then nothing. In psychological terms, it is as though the percipient's mind, having performed the hallucinatory function, reverts to more orthodox perceptual tasks and in doing so terminates the apparition.

In the more credible of these incredible Hitch-Hiker stories, the disappearance is also the cut-off point of the story's paranormal portion. There is no drive to meet bereaved parents, no confrontation with the knowledge that the erstwhile passenger was a spirit – just the fact of the disappearance itself. If the Phantom Hitch-Hiker *is* an hallucination based on some kind of 'communal image' resource (a possibility which will be examined in a moment), why are the possibly evidential episodes only fragmentary – incomplete for want of an address for the witness to follow up?

Theoretically again, there would be little to militate against the idea of an hallucination in which the apparition talks (or seems to talk) to the witness, though as already mentioned, parapsychological documents indicate that ghosts are usually mute or at best laconic. Nor is there any objection to the concept of more than one witness sharing the same simultaneous hallucination, which would have to be so if we take the Montpellier affair with its *four* spectators at face value. During his survey of Society for Psychical Research accounts, Tyrrell discovered no less than 130 cases involving such collective sightings, a number he felt was by no means exhaustive.

There is some credibility in an hallucinatory conversation so persuasive that the motorist subsequently extends his journey to check upon its details at a specific address received during its course. It is less easy to deal with the allegation that this conversation is then validated by leading him to a set of bereaved relatives at that address. Other than amazing coincidence, we should have to postulate that the donor of this accurate information (the Hitch-Hiker) must have been an authentic departed spirit or – a more desperate solution – an hallucination characterized by the witness having sudden access to data irrelevant to him personally and, of course, remote from his normal state of consciousness (a kind of super-ESP). The ghost identified by its address-giving proclivities is, however, not well-supported by evidence, apart from Tom Harber's dozen Blue Bell Hill cases and a few others. Richard Studholme's baffling adventure at the aforementioned locality may, as already postulated in Chapter Four, have been an elaborate and malicious hoax.

The fragmentary encounters are a degree more believable, not because they resemble or mimic the ghosts accepted by parapsychology but because they conform better with what is known regarding the coherence and duration of hallucinatory experiences. Dreams and drug-induced visions do not normally maintain an intelligible narrative line for long periods. If an hallucination, the Hitch-Hiker may fail to develop fully as per folklore image into a ghost which gives an address because this 'crucial' part of the motif imposes too great a strain on the hallucinatory limit; it may threaten the overriding necessity for normality to seem unimpaired. A vanishing passenger, even one who talks in short sentences, may be permissible; for instance, it could utter a warning about dangerous bends already present in the hallucinator's consciousness, as a result of natural motoring caution or because of local belief that a particular spot is especially hazardous. But an hallucination which passes on more personal information may be different; the onus placed on the witness to follow it up (and risk an uncomprehending response from total strangers when he gets to the address the ghost gave him) could be vetoed.

Journeys into the imagination
The vanishing phantom leaves no trace behind it – unlike the folklore varieties, who when occasion demands, can deposit

pieces of seaweed and pools of water in their wake. There can be no physical confirmation of the incident, for the encounter did not take place on a physical plane. The witness, who is of course unaware that his mind has shifted from one level of 'reality' to another, will be doubly confused by the total absence of anything that might constitute proof that he really met a disappearing person; a reader who follows the hallucinatory Hitch-Hiker model will expect nothing else.

For example, is it really any more puzzling that Maurice Goodenough's experience should not be accompanied by a body or by bloodstains and dented bumpers on his vehicle? However tangible the hallucinatory phantasm may have appeared, it was reducible to auditory and visual *mental* effects; it could not produce *physical* results upon solid matter (the car bumper). In this particular instance the strange 'dramatic machinery' just cited might insist on the witness's perceptions registering sense data that enforced the reality of the experience: a moment of impact as the car hit the figure, blood on parts of the victim's body. Hypothetical as this process must remain, it may provide some clues to the interpretation of the Goodenough incident. Whether the hallucination hypothesis can encompass the Blue Bell Hill stories *en bloc* is another question. Moreover, this approach deals only with the machinery behind the experience and not with the contents. Why, for instance, did Mr Goodenough have *this* experience and not some other? If the scenario was based on material from some racial/cultural *gestalt*, why was *this* set of circumstances selected rather than a more typical Hitch-Hiker encounter script? Did the figure have some private or symbolic significance for the driver, a message that was worked out in this peculiar manner? Was it a dramatization of some submerged memory or fear? We lack the biographical (and other) details that would enable us to decide.

The source of an hallucination is not the same thing as its cause. An hallucinatory haunting could be the result of auto-suggestion, as where a susceptible motorist meets a Phantom Hitch-Hiker in a spot like the Barandas turn-off, where local or widely-publicized lore asserts she can be occasionally encountered; other hypotheses speak of hallucinogenic areas where people are uniformly affected by some occult property of the atmos-phere, though direct evidence for these areas and energies is hard to find. Somewhere in the middle – better-evidenced, but still speculative – is the theory that a combination of factors may render certain persons liable to hallucinate.

To explain Hitch-Hiker experiences after this fashion, we

might ponder on the fact that motoring is statistically the most probable or likely cause of premature death faced by most twentieth-century people – hence, a pursuit fraught with an element of sudden danger; that the act of driving requires a minute yet significant alteration of normal consciousness, which over long journeys can lead to a sort of spontaneous dissociation nicknamed 'highway hypnosis', sometimes accompanied by vivid hallucinations; that night driving may involve a form of sensory deprivation which further increases the likelihood of hallucination occurring. Lack of space forbids a more detailed development of these hints and it is vital to add that the odds against any of them leading into an encounter with a disappearing passenger must be astronomical.

The hallucination hypothesis is no more than that – a concept founded upon supposition; how one could subject it to experimental verification defies ingenuity. Nor is it likely to please those who demand a straight answer to the question of whether or not incidents like the Phantom Hitch-Hiker are *real* and *literally* take place.

In refusing to distinguish between the objective and subjective reality of psi events, the psychoanalytical method favoured by Carl Jung and Aniela Jaffé reconciles the dichotomy between a literally real experience and one that is imagined. The ubiquity and general conformity of Hitch-Hiker accounts may indeed be seen as proof of their validity, but to Jaffé such material is more valuable as 'proof of the psychological significance'.[14] Their similarity points to 'primordial, typical forms of feelings and thought that are repeated always and everywhere . . . *archetypes*'.[15] And the value of the archetype in the interpretation of psi phenomena lies, as she sees it, in its ability to do justice to both the objective physical world and the inner, subjective or psychical one; these are not viewed as distinct or irreconcilable, but as 'two different aspects of the same background reality'.[16] In short, they are *both* 'real': the Phantom Hitch-Hiker would be validated as no less so for being a purely psychological phenomenon.

It may be politic to tone down the insistence on the Phantom Hitch-Hiker as an archetype, substituting for that term the word 'image'. Despite its widespread geographical distribution the Hitch-Hiker is not a truly universal symbol, but something that can be adapted to express a special psychological or even spiritual need in almost the same way. Writing in *The Unexplained* on the rationale of how people can see blatantly impossible beings from the wilder shores of folk-tradition, Hilary Evans has suggested the idea of an 'image bank', a vast storehouse of such symbols deposited by racial, cultural and traditional teachings upon which we can unwittingly draw when conditions are apposite.[17]

What *are* these conditions? Why should a particular witness subconsciously select one image at the expense of another? Whether the image be fairy, goblin or Phantom Hitch-Hiker, we are never likely to be able to say. The intimate relationship between ghosts and ghost-seers has, on infrequent occasions, been probed; Nandor Fodor psychoanalyzed the Ash Manor haunting as a mechanism through which the householders expressed their sexual (and other) frustrations, while Edward Osborn showed how the 'Woman in Brown' was composed from the mental complexes of Miss Benson, who saw her at moments of subconsciously-perceived relevance.[18] Not everyone would concede the legitimacy of applying such an analysis to ghosts, however, and even those who do rarely find a chance to apply the hypothesis in the field. It would be fascinating to explore a Phantom Hitch-Hiker incident by way of a psychological profile of its witness, but usually it is a triumph even to encounter such individuals in the flesh, let alone submit them to a lengthy psychological study.

The source of the hallucinatory Hitch-Hiker – if such it is – may correspondingly relate to the durability of the story. 'Of the thousands of psychic experiences – many of them undoubtably true – that have been told orally or in print, what makes the Phantom Hitch-Hiker such a favourite?' asked Cecil de Vada of *Fate Magazine* readers.[19] Attempting to answer his own query, he speculated on the implicit sexuality of the theme: 'I suppose there is no man, celibate or married, who hasn't imagined himself driving on a lonely road at night and being hailed by a glamorous *femme*, even if she is only a wraith.' Ignoring the objection that many Phantom Hitch-Hikers are too elderly to pass for glamorous sex objects, the predominating ratio of male witnesses to female ghosts implies that there may be a grain of truth in this view. Yet the sexual hint remains undeveloped (save in one Mexican tale where the driver actually makes love to the apparition!) and is totally absent in those accounts featuring a male motorist picking up a supposed phantom of the same gender. Nor does the cult of the automobile for its own sake fully explain the appeal of the story and hence (arguably) its accessibility as the source of an hallucination.

I should like to suggest that an emotion less restricted, less basic, may lie behind the allure of the Phantom Hitch-Hiker. Not sexuality nor car-worship, though these may play subsidiary or contributory roles, but a sense of adventure: a timeless adventure, a Romance of the Open Road.

The words 'romance' and 'open road' may have a bitter ring for anyone who has been part of a five-mile traffic jam, yet it is nonetheless true that our modern motoring is related by dynastic ties to the spirit of adventure recurrent throughout narrative traditions of the world. It is prevalent in the medieval ballads, the songs that open conventionally with, 'As I rode out one morning', and in the stories of knights tested by monsters, evil women, faery folk *and* apparitions once the security of home is left behind.

The challenges and perils of the Open Road did not evaporate when literature became more realistic. Novels like *Tom Jones* and *The Pickwick Papers* make use of the same motif, replacing the outrageously supernatural adversaries with human ones. The structure is peculiarly well suited to the American tradition of adventure, travel, self-reliance and danger in the unexplored recesses of a partially conquered land; several critics spotted the use of the picaresque in the 1969 film 'Easy Rider', which essentially concerns the good and bad experiences of two young non-conformist types riding across the southern USA on motorcycles. The adventures of the horsebound knight-at-arms and Tom Jones, and those befalling the motorbike-straddling 'Captain America' and Billy, are not gratuitous devices; they are intended to test and develop the characters of each protagonist. The innate love of motoring for itself can be traced back to some subliminal awareness of this Open Road dream, however formal and unadventurous motoring may have become nowadays.

Witnesses of the Phantom Hitch-Hiker resemble counterparts of the old-time heroes, caught unexpectedly between two places but lacking any conscious awareness of the adventure tradition they partake of. Perhaps under the sensory conditions just outlined the old, half-forgotten folk-motifs, the semi-digested newspaper accounts of years gone by, can come welling into the upper regions of the mind, providing the informational content of the experience: the Phantom Hitch-Hiker, a hallucinatory-real figure evoked when one constituent of the memory operates like a post-hypnotic suggestion. Or perhaps these conditions wipe aside the sophisticated censoring devices of modern civilization, allowing the driver to regress to the status of a medieval adventurer whose personal trial is the Mysterious Companion, one of those delusive denizens of the Other World who attached themselves to lone travellers for the purpose of testing them. The jarring note is that once the experience reaches its climax the witness reverts to being a twentieth-century motorist who, unlike the medieval traveller, has no conscious belief in the world of Faery and who cannot understand the nature of his short-term companion.

Men and women of vision

It seems curious that although we acknowledge that folklore conditions what we believe on a conscious level – reference our faith in the authenticity of 'whale tumour stories' or 'urban legends' – we rarely ponder on how it might simultaneously act at a *sub*conscious one. Over 150 years ago Dr Samuel Hibbert, an arch-critic of paranormal pretensions, took it as understood that hallucinations could evolve from this nebulous source:

In well-authenticated ghost-stories of a supposed supernatural character, ideas, which are rendered so unduly intense as to induce spectral illusions, may be traced to such fantastical objects of prior belief, as are incorporated in the various systems of superstition, which for ages have possessed the minds of the vulgar.[20]

Thus folk traditions and particularly pictorial representations could influence the shape of the 'spectres' which hallucinators saw. Extending this theory beyond the plastic arts, it is quite feasible that oral communications also played (and still play) a role in fleshing out the contents of our hallucinatory experiences. Although Dr Hibbert would not know what to make of all this talk of 'altered' or 'alternative' reality, and despite the fact that his emphasis on the morbidity of the entire process no longer carries conviction, the influence of what he styled the 'various systems of superstition' may be allowed.

It could be argued that the folklore entity in question – ghost, goblin, dragon or demon – was never real but thinking made it so; that decade upon decade of belief in such shadow shapes, deposited time after time in the collective and cultural traditions of a race, or even of different races, became a potent suggestive force that affected the way people perceived reality. Like a long dormant hypnotic instruction, it could surge into actuality when individuals were temporarily in the right mental state and the right set of circumstances to be susceptible to it.

In the latter stages of his book, G. N. M. Tyrrell speculates that hauntings for which no living mind could be held (telepathically) responsible might be attributed to the collective 'idea patterns' of popular tradition. He illustrated this thesis by citing some once powerful motifs which for the modern world have lost most of their imaginative force: the god Pan and the fairies, both reputed to be haunters of lonely spots. As the writer intended it, the hypothesis is very relevant to the more numerous accounts of apparitions. The memory of Pan, the fairies *or* a ghost believed to be visible in some certain locality, a folk tradition sunk deep within the levels of personality amid the people in that vicinity, could become accessible to some individuals – those who bore an unconscious awareness of the motif. Given certain conditions, this mental state might reach over from the world of the imagination and be registered in our physical world as a fact.

Allowing for the Phantom Hitch-Hiker's levels of penetration – few ghost stories are so well or so widely known in this day and age – it is not necessary to expect sightings to be confined to special spots of 'haunted' designation. Persons in vastly separated parts of the world, driving on roads untouched by rumours of hauntings and tragedies, would share access to the same old motif; affected by common sensory phenomena, possessed by common psychological needs, wishes, fears or preoccupations, they might also share similar hallucinations. This answers the question as to why or how people across the face of the Earth could hallucinate the same things; and as Tyrrell saw, it would also explain the universality, durability and vitality of certain fantastic apparition legends, whose recurrence surpasses what the power of oral tradition can account for alone.

Pan and the fairies have lost most of their command over the collective imagination of mankind, yet for some reason – and almost against the odds – ghosts have managed to keep theirs. Few folk-ghosts are so firmly established as the Phantom Hitch-Hiker; is there anyone so well qualified as to assess how deeply entrenched it may be in the racial memory? Developing Tyrrell's surmise, the motif may be available under rare, altered-sensory-state conditions to individuals whose encounters, which have for them all the characteristics of Reality, actually reinforce belief in the old image – because it is 'happening'. Far from being an ossified lump, folklore is providing us (in admittedly reworked form) with the material for experiences which perpetuate the old traditions and motifs. It only takes a chance combination of conditions for these semi-archetypes to emerge, proving to us their living potency.

One reason the Phantom Hitch-Hiker retains its glamour is that the ghost is still useful to us. The motif is not an archaic closed system, but a form adaptable to the needs of the hour. Those needs may be personal, national or spiritual. The Hitch-Hiker has a subordinate role as guardian of the living, as seen most patently in the Berkeley (California) story, where she averts a crash by pulling on the handbrake of the car in which she is travelling;[21] and again in the Franco-Spanish collection where she cautions drivers against the dangers of bends in the road. Here the Hitch-Hiker is presented as a ghostly protector against bodily perils – presumably of a kind which resulted in the loss of her own earthly life (a car accident). Elsewhere the apparition's role is not merely to provide physical reassurance, but spiritual guidance also.

For Nuria Hānsom and Edmoana Toews travelling the ice- and fogbound Alaska Highway in October 1974, the Hitch-Hiker was something between a UFO occupant and a guardian angel, a dweller in the middle-ground betwixt the old world of ghosts and the new-found land of extraterrestrials.[22] 'Gordon' tantalized the women by his apparent weightlessness, his allusive remarks ('Do you believe in angels?') and his ability to vanish outside a motel without leaving tracks in the freshly-fallen snow: he was a Hitch-Hiker, but also a direct answer to the prayer for protection invoked over them before they left a religious convention at the start of their long journey. Truck-driver Hugh Cavalli's vanishing passenger in the Nevada desert (1951, but only told nearly thirty years later!) denied the sarcastic suggestion that he was Jesus Christ, but admitted to being a 'man of vision'; besides the untestable prophecies he made regarding the reclamation of the desert about him, he predicted various things relevant to the driver's future and we are told that in due course these came true.

Apart from demonstrating that Strange Things Happen in this World, that adventures can still unfold on the Open Road, the Hitch-Hiker may take on the duty of spiritual guardian. Not surprisingly, the road-ghost underscores its 'message' by a paranormal feat intended to draw attention to its superior (non-human) status: it vanishes. Occasionally, too, there are a whole series of such proofs. Miracles have ever been regarded as a sign of the performer's spiritual perfection. We can trust the Hitch-Hiker because, unlike ourselves, he can dematerialize from a speeding vehicle, can stand in sub-zero temperatures in just his shirt-sleeves (as did Gordon) or, according to Mr Cavalli's testimony, he can produce a tuna sandwich out of thin air.

Though hardly in the same league as feeding 5000 on five loaves and two small fishes, the latter attempt at providing spiritual credentials shows the ghost-guardian-prophet moving to occupy a yet more religiose position. This is far more clearly expressed when the entity's spiritual purpose is conveyed by simulation of more familiar, conventional symbols of faith –

where it appears as a heavenly messenger, an angelic pedestrian, and even as Jesus Christ incarnate.

Professor Lydia Fish of the State University of Buffalo had no trouble in identifying the folk-origins of 'Jesus on the Thruway'. This New York hitcher in hippie guise who prophesied to drivers of the Second Coming before vanishing (sometimes without stopping to unbuckle his seat-belt) appeared in a large collection of tales coinciding with the religious revival on university campuses, an obvious corollary of the Jesus Christ Superstar quasi-cult.[23] William A. Wilson detected the hitch-hiking phantom masquerading as one of the Three Nephites of Mormon lore, ancient disciples permitted to remain on earth and 'show themselves to whatsoever man it seemeth them good'. Here the upgraded ghost advised the elect (members of the Church) to stock up with one and later two years' supplies against the economic depression – more recently, against the aftermath of nuclear war.[24]

Religious doubt or neurosis may have given birth to the old lady who predicted the destruction of Milan – a convenient symbol of Italian materialism? – in 1977.[25] Uncertainty of another kind was general in the Pacific States following the eruption of Mount St Helens on 18 May 1980; within a month police in Tacoma, Washington had received up to twenty calls concerning a 'Woman of Doom' who moved from indefinite prophecies on the end of the world theme to an item of more local interest: the troublesome volcano was due to blow up again on 18 June.

In point of fact, Mount St Helens *did* experience some volcanic activity in June – and again in July – but the apocalyptic promises of the ghastly old woman were not kept. In subsequent excursions she was transformed to a more attractive female in a white gown and the new schedule for destruction of everything within a radius of 100 miles was 12 October. Again her prophetic powers seemed less amazing than her ability to vacate the back seat of a car travelling at 60 m.p.h. – the Mount steamed dreadfully throughout the month, but once more the region was spared.

As far as these prophecies go, it is self-evident that the people of Washington can place more trust in the recording equipment installed by geophysicists than in supernatural hitch-hiking oracles who reinforce the truth of their statements by vanishing. That these predictions fall flat is as inevitable as the failure of *The Oregonian's* reporter Dan Hortsch and the editor of Hawaii's Fortean publication *Full Moon*, Jacob Davidson, to trace actual witnesses who had encountered the itinerant prophetess.[26] It is more realistic here to abandon the para-psychologist's endeavour to pin down such specificities and to inquire what these scare stories may mean.

Aniela Jaffé would have us believe that such narratives 'need not be regarded as objective proof of the experience reported, but [their ubiquity] might well be regarded as proof of the psychological significance of this type of experience'.[27] That is, the fact they are told, independent of whatever level of reality they operate on, signifies a genuine need: but what precisely is the character of that need?

These prophetic Phantom Hitch-Hikers *are* men and women of vision, but that vision is our own. They voice our personal wishes, fears, preoccupations. Small wonder, then, that events rarely prove them to be better at seeing into the future than we are. Of itself, the resurgence of the Version B Hitch-Hiker in the 1970s – at the expense, it seems, of the more traditional model, where the phenomenon is a mere departed spirit – may signify that we have little hope regarding what lies in store for us. It is somehow easier, more full of impact, to have a supernatural being express this *weltschmerz* than to say it out loud ourselves.

For members of specific religious persuasions, though, the message may emphasize the teachings of the particular faith to which the witness, the narrator, the listener of the tale adheres. Even when that message reflects a fundamentally pessimistic vision of the future (the city, the region, the world is to be destroyed because of Man's spiritual misdemeanours) there is a note of hope for the elect, the Church member, the true follower: he/she/they will be saved, the Faith vindicated. The Hitch-Hiker is here a token of some Higher Power's merciful interest. Belief in the omen reaffirms one's belief in the doctrines of whatever religious path you follow. As one confessed believer in Little Rock's highway apostle put it: 'I guess it could be folklore. But I am a Christian and would like to think it is true.'[28]

In this way the Phantom Hitch-Hiker – legend, ghost, image, symbol – fades effortlessly back into the chiaroscuro demesne of folklore, its natural home. The main difficulty in discussing the evidence that this road-ghost cum heavenly messenger ever ventures out into the objectively-experienced world of humanity lies in the ease with which it commutes between fact and fiction.

This book has made the unavoidable concession that there is sound evidence pointing to the Phantom Hitch-Hiker being a classic fabrication – a supernatural tale told as a matter of truth because that is part of the narrative convention. Outside that convention, the story is obviously *not* true: a folk-ghost, 'whale tumour', urban legend. It has also suggested there is evidence that closer examination reveals incidents which may rest on something more solid: genuine-sounding apparitional encounters, vague and inexplicit as the phase must remain. That evidence is no stronger but certainly no weaker than applies in some cases of ghost-seeing which, by parapsychological concensus, are authenticated and therefore valid.

Fact sometimes follows fiction; fiction can take fact and improve upon it. Are these truncated stories of vanishing passengers imperfect versions of the *old* story – or is the old story a fragmentary episode onto which a meaningful conclusion was tacked by some skilful narrator?

A motorist goes into a police station to report that he has just picked up a hitch-hiker who in short order vanished from the travelling vehicle. The police believe him – at least, they believe him enough to spend time fruitlessly following up his report. We could sit back and be entertained and then dismiss the tale. Or we could verify, first that such a report was made and second that the police acted as the story-line asserts. Should both allegations prove true, we can still dismiss the thing: police involvement or not, there is still absolutely no guarantee that the witness was speaking the truth. And even if he *was*, the truth as he perceived it may not correspond with the truth of what actually happened.

We might reject the tale, not because it is too much like something we have heard or read before, but because it is impossible. *All* ghost stories feature impossibilities and in this one, where the validity of the evidence is known only to the solitary witness, it may seem safer to avoid the issue of reconciling the contradiction that for this individual the impossible is said to have happened.

Meanwhile the Phantom Hitch-Hiker, genuine ghost or old story, is out there somewhere – inside our minds somewhere – waiting for the approach of night . . . and a motorist.

NOTES AND REFERENCES

Chapter One

1 Quotes here are from Sally Staples' 'Was it a Ghost that hitched a lift and . . .?', *Sunday Express*, 21 October 1979. The full provenance of the story (and of course more details) appears in Chapter Five of this book.

2 'Thumbs down to ghostly hiker' (by George Edwards), *News of the World*, 13 April 1975; 'Luigi takes a ghostly ride' (by Paul House, Rome), *Sunday People*, 11 March 1973; 'Was that a ghost sitting on the speed cop's pillion seat?' (Prakash Chandra, New Delhi, based on material in *Musawat*, Pakistan), see *Sunday Express*, 2 December 1979, and cf. *Psychic News*, 8 December 1979 ('Ghost Takes Him for a Ride'). All three incidents are more fully described in later chapters.

3 'Mystery of the Beautiful Hitch-Hiker', *Weekend*, 29 November-5 December 1978, p.30.

4. London: Duckworth, 1933. See pp.227-229.

5. The Hitch-Hiker canon contains a whole subdivision in which the ghost is encountered away from the roadside and draws attention to herself in a way that guarantees she gets a lift without having to ask for one (see remarks on the C-variant in Chapter Two.)

6 The italics are mine.

7 'Ghost Walks After Crash', *Sunday People*, 14 July 1974.

8 Footnote to Crookes' 'Some Further Experiments on Psychic Force', *Quarterly Journal of Science*, 1 October 1871.

9 'La Dame Blanche où quand l'auto-stoppeuse se volatilise' – see *LDLN* March/April 1982. The writer cites several French newspaper reports of this incident, *viz. Midi Libre*, 28 May 1981, *France Soir*, 29 May 1981, and *France Dimanche* and *Le Journal de Montpellier*, for June 8-14 and 29 May-4 June 1981 respectively.

10 *Lumières dans la Nuit*, March 1978.

11 Charles Fort, *Lo!* (London: Victor Gollancz, 1931), p.90.

12 This summary combines versions in the *Sunday Express*, 14 August

1977 and *The Weekly News*, 20 August 1977. Other sources are studied during the more detailed survey of this case in Chapter Three.

13 I have the story of Resurrection Mary from Steve Moore's summary in *Fortean Times*, 24, pp.13-14. Steve in turn collected it from the *Chicago Sun-Times* of 9 August 1975, which was reporting on a paper read by Richard T. Crowe at the 1975 Chicago Fortfest. Paul Screeton ('Tales of phantom hitch-hikers', *The Mail*, Hartlepool, 31 October 1980, p.27) adds that Mary's destination is Archer Street.

14 The Weeping Girl of Southampton appears in Wendy Boase's *The Folklore of Hampshire and the Isle of Wight* (London: B. T. Batsford Ltd., 1976), pp.89-90.

15 The bridal quartet of Blue Bell Hill sounds oddly similarly to the four bridesmaids said by Mr Jack Hallam to haunt a road outside Great Melton, Norfolk. (*The Ghost's Who's Who*, David and Charles, 1977, p.24). They were, of course, Tragic Accident casualties – their coachman ran the vehicle in which they were travelling into a pool. The complexities of assessing the relevance of the car crash explanation in the Blue Bell Hill case will be seen in Chapter Six.

16 Lewis Carroll, *Alice's Adventures in Wonderland*, Chapter XII ('Alice's Evidence').

17 For instance, Le Fanu's 'Authentic Narrative . . .' (*Dublin University Magazine* October 1862) could be compared with Joseph Proctor's story of the Willington Mill haunting in the *Journal of the Society for Psychical Research*, 1891/92.

18 Andrew Lang, *The Book of Dreams and Ghosts* (London: Longmans, Green and Co., new impression, 1899). See Preface to First Edition, p.viii.

19 Lang, *ibid.* pp.15-16.

Chapter Two
1 Indiana University Folklore Series, No.20 (The Hague: Mouton and Co., 1966). See especially pp.147-149.

2 Louis C. Jones, 'Hitchhiking Ghosts in New York', *California Folklore Quarterly*, III, 4 (October 1944), p.284.

3 The relevant papers are: 'The Vanishing Hitchhiker', *California Folklore Quarterly*, I, 4 (October 1942), pp.303-335, and 'A History of the Vanishing Hitchhiker', ditto II, 1 (January 1943), pp.13-25.

4 Beardsley and Hankey, 'The Vanishing Hitchhiker', *op.cit.*, p.305.

5 *Ibid.*

6 In 1946 Mother Frances Cabrini became the first (naturalized) US citizen to be canonized. Jones states that the 'B' stories ceased to be heard in New York after Fall 1943. Readers' attention is also

drawn to his remarks on a parallel motif current at this time where the Hitch-Hiker's prophecy on the end of the war is sworn to be as true as the fact that the car he/she travels in will be carrying a corpse by the end of the day. (And of course, by a curious concatenation of events, it does perform that function.) Jones terms these BX Versions.

7 *Fortean Times*, 21 (1977). See pp.32-33.

8 The reference to the Hitch-Hiker discoursing on the fate of the American Embassy hostages appeared in the *Indiana Star's* summary (26 July 1980) of an alleged incident near Pine Bluff. The informant said she had the story from a woman whose parents (plus another couple) were involved.

9 A sample of contemporary press treatments (*Indiana Star, Arkansas Gazette,* etc.) was subsequently reprinted in the Hawaiian magazine *Full Moon* 1: 2 (August/September 1980), edited by Jacob Davidson.

10 Jeffrey Blyth's report on 'Riddle of car-hitch traveller', *Sunday People*, 10 August 1980, p.5.

11 Aside from borrowed clothing, these 'proof items' come in all shapes and sizes and need not be articles of apparel. Beardsley and Hankey's sample reveals several other types of token left by the girl in devious, presumably deliberate, carelessness as she vacates the vehicle, including baggage, books *and* a piece of seaweed. The last was corroboration that the Hitch-Hiker in the Hawaiian tale was the spirit of a girl drowned off the beach where the man originally encountered her. Naturally enough, the seat she occupied was wet too – providing a parallel with a story from Waterlooville, Hampshire, given in Joan Forman's *The Haunted South* (London: Robert Hale and Co., 1968; see p.108). The writer makes the inspired quip that she has come upon many tales of ghostly hitch-hikers, but 'not until now one who left a wet imprint behind, or the imprint of a wet behind'.

12 The *Sunday People* article is summarized by Paul Screeton in his 'Tales of phantom hitch-hikers', (Hartlepool: *The Mail*, 31 October 1980, p.27).

13 In another newspaper account (source uncertain, date *c.*June 1973) Lucia is described as a pretty blonde who died *four* years ago and the named witness (still a motor cyclist) is Mario Scotti, who loans her a *jacket*. Later this is found on her grave and there is the same Identification-by-Picture at the deceased's address. Police are said to have verified the story.

14 Written by Addington and Harman, 'Laurie' was released by EM Long and Golddust Records. The BBC Gramophone Library, which knows of two recorded versions (by Dickey Lee and by Keith Kelly respectively), received their copies in June and July 1965.

15 Preternatural lightness of the Hitch-Hiker was one feature of a
   c. 1930 story from Mountain Home as told by Tom Shiras to Vance
   Randolph, who recorded it in his 'Folktales from Arkansas', *Journal
   of American Folklore*, Vol.65 (1952), pp.159-166.

16 Jones, *op.cit.*, p.286.

17 Jacqueline Simpson, *The Folklore of Sussex* (London: B. T. Batsford
   Ltd., 1973). See pp.50-51.

18 Beardsley and Hankey, 'The Vanishing Hitchhiker', *op.cit.*, p.308.

19 Beardsley and Hankey, 'The History of the Vanishing Hitchhiker',
   op.cit., p.13.

20 *Ibid.*, p.14.

21 *Ibid.*, p.16.

22 *Ibid.* p.22.

23 See pp. 16-18.

24 For example, the ghost is not met by the roadside and gets a lift
   without actually asking for one – both Version C characteristics.
   As Sutro died in 1933, there is a chance that his story predates
   those noted by Beardsley and Hankey, but it could resemble their
   Version Cs by chance rather than by intention.

25 Andrew MacKenzie, *Dracula Country. Travels and Folk Beliefs in
   Romania* (London: Arthur Barker Ltd., 1977). See pp.87-88.

26 *The New Suffolk Garland. A Miscellany of Anecdotes, Romantic Ballads...
   Collected, compiled and edited by John Glyde, Jun.* (Ipswich: printed for
   the author; London: Simpkin, Marshall and Co., 1866). See
   pp.216-220.

27 Louis C. Jones, *op.cit.*, p.292. Further, in societies where walking is
   the prevailing mode of travel there are tales in which the hero
   conducts the ghost of a girl who disappears at her home – Phantom
   Hitch-Hikers in all but the act of getting a lift. Jones cites a Chinese
   story of this kind in Jon Lee's *The Golden Mountain* (San Francisco:
   WPA, 1940).

28 *Folk-Lore. Transactions of the Folk-Lore Society*, Vol. XVIII, No.4 (31
   December 1907), pp.376-390.

29 *Ibid.*, p.376.

30 Philip Brandt George, 'The Ghost of Cline Avenue: "La Llorona"
   in the Calumet Region', *Indiana Folklore*, V, 1 (1972), pp.56-91.

31 *The Vanishing Hitchhiker. Urban Legends and their Meanings.* (London:
   Pan Books Ltd., 1983). See pp.28-29.

32 Beardsley and Hankey, 'The Vanishing Hitchhiker', *op.cit.*, p.305.

33 Rodney Dale, *The Tumour in the Whale. A Collection of Modern Myths* (London: Universal, 1978). A 'Whale Tumour Story' (WTS) is the term coined by George Melly for an apocryphal, unlikely, often macabre or accidentally humorous tale that the teller insists is perfectly true on the 'evidence' that it befell someone he knew or a friend of a friend (foaf). As Mr Dale remarks, many a ghostly episode is a WTS; only lack of space may have spared the Phantom Hitch-Hiker from finding a niche in his chapter on specimens of the genre from the world of motoring.

34 Footnote to the story of how Egyptian engine-drivers made their trains run better by stoking up the furnaces with the mummies of Pharaohs (*The Innocents Abroad*, Chapter 58).

35 A paraphrase of a remark made by D. J. West, 'The Investigation of Spontaneous Cases', *Proc. Soc. for Psychical Research*, XLVIII, Part 175 (July 1948), p.274.

36 Lang, *Book of Dreams and Ghosts* (1899 edn.), p.174.

37 Brunvand, *op.cit.*, pp.28-29.

38 Beardsley and Hankey, 'The Vanishing Hitchhiker', *op.cit.*, p.309.

39. *Ibid.*, p.310.

40 See Margo Skinner, 'The Vanishing Hitchhiker Again', *Western Folklore*, 12, 1 (January 1953), pp.136-137 for a comparable case from La Porte, Indiana.

41 The Mouse in the Coke Bottle motif receives detailed treatment in Professor Brunvand's book (*op.cit.*), pp.71ff. See also Chapter Four.

Chapter Three

1 For a very readable illustrated guide to the history of the village, see Michael McGarvie's *Nunney and Trudoxhill: An Historical Sketch* (published by the Nunney Silver Jubilee Committee, 1977).

2 Reluctantly, but by request, I am withholding the real name of the witness.

3 *Fortean Times*, 24 (Winter 1978), 'Ghosts and Visions'; see pp.13-14.

4 *Sunday Express*, 21 August 1977. See Letters, p.4.

5 *Bath and West Evening Chronicle*, 30 August 1977. Also mentioned in *Fortean Times*, 24 (see Note 3 above).

6 Abson Wick, Bristol: Abson Books, 1976. See p.36 ('The Phantom Hiker').

7 Ms Royal gave an identical (but briefer) summary of the story in an interview with reporter Jack Pleasant two years later; see *Reveille*, 13 January 1978.

8   E.g., the *Bath and West Evening Chronicle* variously stated the phantom made its first appearance 'last year' (in issue of 4 August 1977; see 'Ghoul of the Road. Phantom who hitches lifts' on p.8), or again that he had been baffling police and villagers 'for years' (article entitled 'The ghost rider of Nunney runs into a hitch', issue for Tuesday 23 August 1977, p.4).

9   'The ghost rider of Nunney runs into a hitch', *Bath and West Evening Chronicle*, 23 August 1977, p.4.

10 The Frome Town Guide says that Murder Combe was known by this name as far back as AD 942, when it was mentioned as a boundary of land granted by King Edmund to Earl Athelstan.

11 Kingsley Palmer, *The Folklore of Somerset*. (London: B. T. Batsford Ltd., 1976), p.136.

12 'The hitch-hiking ghost of Nunney is bad for trade', *Somerset Standard*, 5 August 1977.

13 E.g., the *Bath and West Evening Chronicle*, 4 August 1977 speaks of it happening 'earlier *this* year' (my italics).

14 This comes from an oral informant.

15 *Bath and West Evening Chronicle*, 4 August 1977; *The Weekly News*, 20 August 1977. (See also p.25).

Chapter Four

1   Jung's Foreword to Aniela Jaffé's *Apparitions and Precognition. A Study from the Point of View of C. G. Jung's Analytical Psychology* (New York: University Books, Inc. 1963). See pp.vii-viii.

2   Aniela Jaffé, *op.cit.*; see pp.181-183. The section is signficantly entitled 'Fictitious Stories'.

3   See 'Ghost Mystery for Couple in Ockendon Lane' (actually, in Dennises Lane), *Thurrock Gazette*, 25 February 1977. The sequel ('The Night the "ghosts" posed for the Gazette', by Mick Pulfrey, with photograph by David Henderson) appeared in the same paper of 4 March 1977.

4   As is firmly indicated by a clipping sent to me by the *Kent Messenger* Information Unit: 'Two in "haunting" encounter on Blue Bell Hill' dated 30 August 1977. The story appeared in briefer form in the *London Evening News* of 12 September 1977.

5   Peter Moss, *Ghosts Over England* (London: Elm Tree Books/Hamish Hamilton in association with Book Club Associates, 1977; Sphere paperback edition, 1979). See Sphere edn., pp.146-148. Mr Unsworth's letter originally appeared in Dexon's 'Western Ways' column of the *Exeter Express and Echo* for 12 August 1970, p.6, under the title 'The Night a Ghost hitched a Lift'. Peter Moss's version – collated, he says, from diverse sources – adds a few details or inferences not given in this earlier report. My summary is based

upon this, but with certain adjustments taking into consideration the Exeter paper's account.

6 As a point of interest, another A38 spectral jaywalker – a *woman* in a white coat, this time, but haunting the Barrow Gurney stretch closer to Bristol – appears in Royal and Girvan's *Local Ghosts*, p.30. (For publication details, see Note 6 to Ch.3).

7 See also *Exeter Express and Echo*, 5 August 1970 ('Ghost of the A38 has been seen again').

8 See footnote 5 above. 'Dexon' notes that the Unsworth Hitch-Hiker seems to be identical with the figure Mrs Swithenbank narrowly avoided hitting.

9 Vern Robinson, 'Ubiquitous Hitchhiker', *Western Folklore*, 14, 3 (July 1955), p.215.

10 Jan Harold Brunvand, *op.cit.*, p.33.

11 'I Gave A Ghost A Lift, Says Pop Star', see p.2. Also abstracted in *The News* (now *Fortean Times*), 10, p.5, and summarized in Paul Screeton's 'Tales of phantom hitch-hikers'. (*The Mail*, Hartlepool, 31 October 1980, p.27), which cites the Maurice Goodenough encounter in this context.

12 'Blueberry Hill' is presumably a slip of the journalistic pen. I recently confirmed with a relation of Mr Studholme's that the incident described above took place on Blue *Bell*, not Blueberry, Hill.

Chapter Five

1 'Night Ride Riddle of Hitch-Hike Ghost', by Anne Court, *Dunstable Gazette*, 18 October 1979, p.7. A freely-adapted version of Roy Fulton's adventure, complete with imagined dialogue, appears in Nigel Blundell and Denis Boar's *The World's Greatest Ghosts* (Octopus Books, 1983), pp.129-130.

2 Telephone conversation of 9 May 1983.

3 See p.11.

Chapter Six

1 See the chapter on 'Early Man' by George Clinch in *The Victoria County History of the County of Kent* (London: Archibald Constable and Company Limited, 1908), Vol.II, p.319.

2 *The Gazette* (formerly the *Maidstone Gazette*, but published under this new title since 1970), 16 July 1974. See 'Hunt for phantom schoolgirl road victim'.

3 'Hitch-Hiker Killed', *Maidstone Gazette*, Tuesday 13 August 1968, front page.

4 'Have You Met the Ghostly Hitch-Hiker?'

5   This useful clipping and many others came from the *Kent Messenger* Information Unit's files. The name of the paper in which it appeared was missing, but it is dated 9 December 1970.

6   'Girls die in wedding eve smash', *Maidstone Gazette*, Tuesday 23 November 1965, front page. Another clipping courtesy of the *Kent Messenger* Information Unit dated 29 November 1965 records the death of the bride-to-be. Both articles are by Peter Rimmer. Another source suggests the age of the victim may have been 24, not 22.

7   London: Robert Hale, 1978. See pp.21-23.

8   These cuttings, entitled 'Drivers beware of the phantom on the hill' and 'Spectre of Bluebell [*sic*] Hill', are dated 19 and 26 July 1974 respectively.

9   The printed sources for this account are *The News of the World* and *Sunday People* of 14 July 1974 and various *Kent Messenger* group papers for 15, 19 and 26 July 1974.

10 *Op.cit.*, 19 and 26 July 1974.

11 Some newspapers spoke of 'tracker dogs', but a letter from Kent County Constabulary shows that only one was employed in the search. (Letter to the author, 19 February 1980.)

12 *The Gazette*, 2 April 1974, front page.

13 Roy Plaskett's 'What a Story – if it's on the level!', *Kent Messenger*, 26 September 1980, p.6. His summary mentions two Maidstone-bound males as witnesses and he concludes that the journalist has a duty to chase up such tales because, after all, truth is often stranger than fiction – 'Unless, of course, he has heard it all before!'.

Chapter Seven

1   Beardsley and Hankey, 'The Vanishing Hitchhiker', *op.cit.*, p.305.

2   *Ibid.*

3   See p.27.

4   As told by Ms Theo Brown, folklore recorder for the Devonshire Association, and mentioned in Mr Sam Richards' article 'Ghostly Hitch-Hiker', *Western Morning News*, 10 March 1972. Ms Brown told me in a letter (26 January 1980) that she first heard this tale about 20 years ago.

5   See p.12 and footnote 2 to Chapter 1.

6   '"Motorcycle ghost" makes its presence felt', *Middlesex News* (Framlingham, Mass., USA), 11 April 1980, p.1. This UPI dispatch appeared (with minor amendments of phrase) in *The Trentonian* (New Jersey) of the same date, as reprinted in *Pursuit Magazine*, Summer 1980. Jerome Clark's 'Update' column in *Fate Magazine* (August 1980, p.78) contains a summary; David Barritt's *Scope*

article – see following note – does likewise. The Fraser sighting (Good Friday 1973) also appears in the Barritt piece.

7   My two sources are: 'Girl-Ghost Hitches Ride', by Cynthia Hind, *Fate Magazine* (July 1979, pp.54-59), with two photographs and sketch map; and David Barritt's 'The Phantom Hitch-Hiker', in *Scope* (South Africa), 18 July 1980, pp.54-57, 59, which is photo-illustrated. Finally, I believe the Uniondale case was summarized as 'The Baffling Case of the Hitchhiking Ghost', in *The National Enquirer* (USA), 4 July 1978.

8   Lavater, *op.cit.*, 'The First Part', Chap.XIX (Oxford edn., p.96).

9   *Ibid.*, p.88.

10 Louis C. Jones, *op.cit.*, pp.289ff.

11 See page 15.This description of the *langsuyar* follows that of Hasi Mohtar Bin in *The Bomah and the Hantu* (Kuala Lumpur: Federal Publications, 1979; see pp.8-9). The *langsuyar* (or *langsuir*) was originally considered the ghost of a beautiful woman who sucked the blood of children. (Walter William Skeat, *Malay Magic*, New York and London: Macmillan and Co., 1900; see pp.325-327). Once again the Phantom Hitch-Hiker appears to have been identified with an older motif and the vampire element softened – the motorist retains his blood, but usually spends several days in fever, in bed or both.

12 'The Devil and the Coachman' can be found in *Ballads Old and New*, compiled and edited by S. H. Atkins (London: Hulton Educational Publications Ltd., 1968; see pp.21-23). It may be permissible to speculate about the satirical message of the 'experience'; did the balladeer mean his reference to the Devil holding a roll of parchment to be seen as a dig at 'devilish' lawyers for instance? If not a satire on some contemporary incident, the ballad could mimic seventeenth-century 'true relations' of ghosts for generalized satiric purposes.

13 G. N. M. Tyrrell, *Apparitions* (published under the auspices of the Society for Psychical Research by Gerald Duckworth and Co. Limited. See revised issue of 1953, especially pp.77-80).

14 Aniela Jaffé, *op. cit.*, p.12.

15 *Ibid.*

16 *Ibid.*, p.205.

17 Hilary Evans, 'The Unexplored Realm', *The Unexplained* (Orbis partwork), No.111. See especially pp.2212-2213.

18 Nandor Fodor, *The Haunted Mind: a Psychoanalyst Looks at the Supernatural* (New York: Helix Press, 1959), see pp.134-172. Edward Osborn, 'The Woman in Brown', *Jnl. Soc. for Psychical Research*, 35, 655 (November-December 1949), pp.123-153. Of

course, both cases were a good deal more complicated than my summary would suggest.

19 'The Phantom Hitchhiker', *Fate Magazine*, August 1968, p.90.

20 Dr Samuel Hibbert, *Sketches of the Philosophy of Apparitions, or, An Attempt to Trace such Illusions to their Physical Causes* (Edinburgh: Oliver and Boyd; London: Geo. B. Whittaker, 2nd. enlarged edition, 1825). See p.125.

21 Beardsley and Hankey, 'The Vanishing Hitchhiker', *op.cit.* See their eighth example (p.320). The interpretation of the San Bernadino pedestrian as a messenger of danger ahead also fits into this subtype: see p.86.

22 'The UFOs that led us Home', by Edmoana Toews, as told to Joseph J. Brewer, *Fate Magazine* June *and* July 1977, pp.38-45, 63-69 respectively (illustrated).

23 Lydia M. Fish, 'Jesus on the Thruway: The Vanishing Hitchhiker Strikes Again', *Indiana Folklore* IX, No.1 (1976), pp.5-13.

24 William A. Wilson, '"The Vanishing Hitchhiker" Among the Mormons', *Indiana Folklore* III, Nos.1/2 (1975), pp.79-97. The basic motif is also discussed in his 'Mormon Legends of the Three Nephites collected at Indiana University', *Indiana Folklore* II, No.1 (1969); see pp.24-27.

25 See pp. 38-39.

26 Miscellaneous coverage of the 'Woman of Doom' – and Hugh Cavalli's belatedly-told account of the 'Man of Vision' mentioned on p.140 – are conveniently reprinted in Jacob Davidson's *Full Moon* (Vol.1, No.2, August/September 1980). For later installment, see also the *Seattle Post-Intelligencer*, 23 September 1980 ('"Goddess" warns of Eruption – then Vanishes') and the *Indiana Star*, 10 October 1980, p.10 ('St Helens Vibrations on Increase').

27 Jaffé, *op.cit.*, p.12.

28 *Arkansas Gazette* ('Mystery of Vanishing Hitchhiker. Folklore Dating from 19th Century'), 28 July 1980.

BIBLIOGRAPHY

BEARDSLEY, Richard K., and HANKEY, Rosalie.
'The Vanishing Hitchhiker', *California Folklore Quarterly*, 1: 4 (October 1942), pp.303-335.

BEARDSLEY, Richard, and HANKEY, Rosalie.
'A History of the Vanishing Hitchhiker', *California Folklore Quarterly*, 2: 1 (January 1943), pp.13-25.

BRUNVAND, Jan Harold.
The Vanishing Hitchhiker. American Urban Legends and Their Meanings (London: Pan Books Ltd., 1983). See particularly pp.30-45.

DANIELSON, Larry.
'Towards the Analysis of Vernacular Texts: The Supernatural Narrative in Oral and Popular Print Sources', *Journal of the Folklore Institute* (Indiana University), 16: 3 (September/December 1979), pp.130-154.

DAVIDSON, Jacob (ed.).
'The Phantom Hitch-Hiker', *Full Moon: A Report from the Islands* (Hawaii) 1:2 (August/September 1980), pp.1, 5-6, 10.

FISH, Lydia M.
'Jesus on the Thruway: The Vanishing Hitchhiker Strikes Again', *Indiana Folklore*, IX: 1 (1976), pp.5-13.

FONDA, Jesse.
'I Met the Real Phantom Hitchhiker', *Fate Magazine* (January 1977), pp.55-57.

GEORGE, Philip Brandt.
'The Ghost of Cline Avenue: "La Llorona" in the Calumet Region', *Indiana Folklore*, V: 1 (1972), pp.56-91.

JAFFÉ, Aniela.
Apparitions and Precognition. A Study from the Viewpoint of C. G. Jung's Analytical Psychology (New York: University Book, Inc., 1963).

JONES, Louis C.
'Hitchhiking Ghosts in New York', *California Folklore Quarterly*, 3: 4 (October 1944), pp.284-292. See also Ch.6, 'Ghostly Hitchhikers', in his *Things that Go Bump in the Night* (New York: Hill and Wang, 1959).

LANG, Andrew.
The Book of Dreams and Ghosts (London, etc.: Longmans, Green and Co., new impression, 1899).

LUOMALA, Katherine.
'Disintegration and Regeneration: the Hawaiian Phantom Hitchhiker Legend', *Fabula*, 13 (1972), pp.20-59. Reprinted in *Full Moon*, 1:2, 1:3/4, etc., for 1980/81.

SIEGEL, R. K., and WEST, L. J. (eds.).
Hallucinations. Behaviour, Experience and Theory (New York, London, etc.: John Wiley and Sons, 1975).

TOEWS, Edmoana (as told to Joseph J. Brewer).
'The UFOs that led us home', *Fate Magazine* (June and July 1977), pp.38-45, 63-69 respectively.

TYRRELL, G. N. M.
Apparitions (London: published under the auspices of the Society for Psychical Research by Gerald Duckworth & Co. Ltd., rev. edn. 1953).

WILSON, William A.
'"The Vanishing Hitchhiker" among the Mormons', *Indiana Folklore*, III: 1/2 (1975), pp.79-97.

INDEX